INDEPENDENT AND UNOFFICIAL

MINECRAFT
MASTER BUILDER

MEGA METROPOLIS

THIS IS A MORTIMER CHILDREN'S BOOK

Published in 2020 by Mortimer Children's Books
An imprint of Welbeck Children's Limited,
part of Welbeck Publishing Group
20 Mortimer Street, London W1T 3JW

Text and illustrations © Welbeck Children's Limited 2020,
part of Welbeck Publishing Group

ISBN: 978 1 83935 033 7

Designed and packaged by: Dynamo Limited
Written by: Anne Rooney
Build contributors: Jamie Harvey, Darcy Miles, Ben Westwood
Managing Art Director: Matt Drew
Executive Editor: Bryony Davies
Production: Nicola Davey

Printed in Dongguan, China
8 7 6 5 4 3 2 1

The publishers would like to thank the following sources for their kind permission to
reproduce the pictures in this book. Key: T=top, B=bottom, L=left, R=right & C=center.

Baycrest – Wikipedia user – CC-BY-SA-2.5: 67

Getty Images: /Jeffrey Greenberg/Universal Images Group: 106B; /Fuhito Kanayama/
The Image Bank: 186; /Kirkikis: 279BR; /David McNew: 142-143; /Robert Nickelsberg:
108; /Spencer Platt: 94

Shutterstock: /Africa Studio: 217L; /AlenKadr: 177BL; /Alvinku: 129; /Andrey_Kuzmin:
177C; /Artorn Thongtukit: 81T; /bellena: 62; /bibiphoto: 53; /Boonchuay Promjiam:
71TC; /Doug Lemke: 199; /Dudarev Mikhail: 266; /elesi: 200-201; /elRoce: 152; /
FrameAngel: 122-123; /givaga: 177L; /Grand Warszawski: 63T; /haryigit: 143T; /HelloRF
Zcool: 102; /Jaromir Chalabala: 137; /Jonathan Lewis: 95B; /Kazitafahnizeer: 241; /
kzww: 240R; /Lifestyle Graphic: 85; /Lisa S.: 263B; /loraks: 244; /Lukas Gojda: 177T; /
MagMac83: 229T; /Manekina Serafima: 71TL, 71TR; /Martin Janecek: 183T, 183C; /
Nicholas Rjabow: 113T; /Nixx Photography: 225R; /PhotoRoman: 229B; /pxl.store:
105TL, 136; /PunyaFamily: 95T; /ra3rn: 217BR; /Rastislav Sedlak SK: 39T, 105BR; /
Rawpixel.com: 106T; /RDFlemming: 267R; /SAPhotog: 278BR; /SeamlessPatterns: 183B;
/Sean Pavone: 36, 170-171; /st-fotograf: 216; /Stokkete: 283; /Tarica: 224; /tovovan:
147; /Tymonko Galyna: 113B; /Vaclav Volrab: 85T; /zhu difeng: 153T

Every effort has been made to acknowledge correctly and contact the source and/
or copyright holder of each picture. Any unintentional errors or omissions will be
corrected in future editions of this book.

INDEPENDENT AND UNOFFICIAL

MINECRAFT
MASTER BUILDER
MEGA METROPOLIS

ANNE ROONEY

JAMIE HARVEY

DARCY MILES

BEN WESTWOOD

MORTIMER

CONTENTS

WELCOME

TO THE WONDERFUL WORLD OF

MINECRAFT!

You probably know all about Minecraft already, right?
If not, don't worry, it's pretty easy to get the hang of.
If you're a complete newbie, download the game
and get mining those blocks to start building.

Courtesy of imgur.com

Once you've learned the basics, this book will help you build
impressive structures that will be the envy of all your friends...

READY?

OKAY, LET'S GET STARTED!

≪ BUILT FOR SUCCESS ≫

Remember to build your Metropolis in Creative mode. Don't make the mistake of trying it in Survival mode—you'd spend all of your time fighting off aggressive mobs and not enough time perfecting the look of your build! And in Creative mode, you don't have the added challenge of having to mine millions of blocks.

Courtesy of cumez.org

Follow the floorplans for each build, and you'll soon see your city and theme park rise from the ground. Each structure is broken down into simple steps, plus there's information about real-life buildings and other things to help you understand the difference between the Minecraft world and the one you live in!

STAYING SAFE ONLINE

Minecraft is one of the most popular games in the world, and we want you to have fun while you're playing it. However, it is just as important to stay safe when you're online.

Top tips for staying safe are:
- turn off chat
- find a child-friendly server
- watch out for viruses and malware
- set a game-play time limit
- tell a trusted adult what you're doing.

STARTING THE GAME

TOP TIP!

Never reveal your first name, last name, address, email, phone number, or school name online. Your avatar username should not include any of these.

If you're new to Minecraft, download the game and set it up for the first time with a parent or guardian. Together you can work through any technical issues you may have. It is important for adults to know what the game is about.

Courtesy of TheApiem

Minecraft has an amazing community—lots of players enjoy collaborating on huge, complex builds. There might be times when you see something that doesn't seem right, but don't worry, there are a few easy ways to deal with it.

You can mute other players so you won't see their messages, or block them so they can't contact you. You can also report them. Minecraft should be a positive experience for everyone.

Never share any account passwords or any personal information, especially if someone is offering something for nothing—the officials at Minecraft HQ state that there's no way to get coins or marketplace content other than through the game.

And remember, the Minecraft team and server moderators will NEVER ask for your password, or personal information like your address, phone number, age, or full name.

MATERIAL WORLD

Materials have different properties.
In Minecraft you can build a bouncy castle
from wool or a water slide from pink clay,
which would never work in the real world.

« A THEME FOR YOUR CITY »

You don't have to make your city look just like ours. You can use different colors and materials. As long as you stick to the basic structure and dimensions so that it all fits and works in the space, you can change the decorations. Your water ride could be a lava ride. Your shopping mall could have a track running through it.

You could give your whole city a theme through its colors and decorations: Halloween, fairyland, fantasy, or sci-fi. It can be anything you like.

dirt

carved
pumpkin

lava
block

TOP TIP!

Using materials that would work in the real world makes your builds look more realistic.

《 ROCK, METAL, 》 WOOD

bricks

In the real world, buildings are made from lots of different materials. Some of the most common types are:

• brick and concrete

• stone (and slate for roofs)

• wood

• metal

You can use all these in Minecraft, too, so it's worth learning a bit about their properties.

polished granite

stone brick

Brick, stone, and concrete are super-hard and strong. Buildings made of these materials don't easily fall down, are not damaged by weather, and don't burn. But they're also heavy, and quite difficult to work with because they are so hard. Bricks and concrete are made in factories, but stone is cut from the ground.

iron bars

iron block

Metal is strong, but flexible. At high temperatures it melts, but it doesn't burn. We usually use metal for the support structures inside buildings made of concrete or brick. Metals conduct electricity and some are magnetic.

acacia
wood
plank

oak
wood
block

spruce
wood plank

Wood is light, easy to work with, and easy to find—it grows on trees! Wood is flammable (it can catch fire). Over time, wood can rot while structures made from brick, stone, and concrete can last for centuries.

oak
wood
plank

In Minecraft, wood comes in blocks, stairs, planks, and slabs, and also forms other items such as fences and doors. Minecraft also offers different types of wood.

wooden
door

oak
fence

oak wood
stair

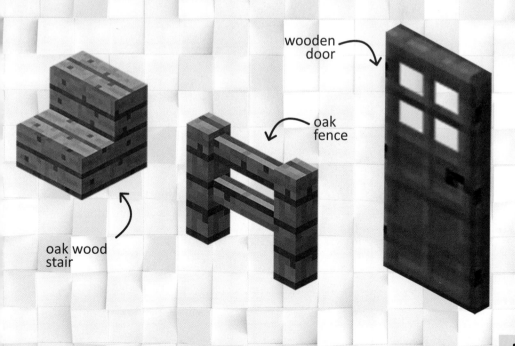

BLOCK-I-PEDIA

Check out all of these cool blocks. You may not need them all for the builds in this book, but you can use your imagination and add them if you expand your city. Have fun experimenting!

DIRT

Dirt is one of the most common types of block in Minecraft and has a range of uses. To avoid storing too much, it can be used to fill in areas ready for other tasks, like farming! It can be found under any layer of grass and best destroyed with a shovel.

GRASS

It's the block that everybody knows and loves! Grass blocks are all over the place in Minecraft and, just like in real life, they require dirt and enough sunlight to grow. Great for any garden, grass can spread and regrow too!

COAL

Blocks of coal can be mined using any of the pickaxes. They can be used as a type of fuel for the furnace, so they're a great block to have if you plan on smelting a lot of your ores.

DIAMOND

Diamond is a very hard block and needs an iron or diamond pickaxe to be mined. It can spawn in "obsidian rooms" and "lava rooms" within woodland mansions. Use diamonds to make your pickaxes really strong.

EMERALD

A bright block of green mineral, emerald is a great block for decoration. It can only be mined using the diamond pickaxe and is very valuable. You can also place one under a note block to create a "bit" sound.

≪ BLOCK-I-PEDIA ≫

SAND

Sand can be found in many places throughout Minecraft. It can be broken without the use of tools, but a shovel is the fastest way to get it. Sand is used to make concrete, so it's very important to your builds.

GOLD

Gold can be used to make armor, tools, and more. It needs a diamond or iron pickaxe to mine and is very expensive, so some players use it in their builds to show how rich they are!

QUARTZ

A quartz block is a mineral which is only used for decoration. It can be mined using any pickaxe and can then be built into chiseled quartz blocks, quartz pillars, or smooth quartz. A great building block.

SNOW

You can use a silk touch enchantment on a shovel to make snow drop itself, or you can use a normal shovel to make it drop snowballs. When snow is in a block it will not melt in high light levels or get destroyed by water. It can also be used to make snow golems!

ICE

Ice can be made by freezing water and will also melt in the sun or near heat blocks. It is a very slippery block which means it can be used in some interesting ways, since it will cause players to slide along at faster than normal speeds.

FROSTED ICE

Just like ice, this block is slightly slippery and will leave behind water when destroyed. It is created when a player walks near water wearing the Frost Walker enhancement.

CLAY

Clay is a versatile building material that can be found near watery places and swamps. It doesn't require any tools to mine it, but a shovel will help you mine it quickest. When smelted with any fuel it can be made into terracotta.

choice of colors

MAGMA

The magma block causes fire damage to players who stand on it because it is incredibly hot, even if the block is underwater. They also give off a low level of light. Mobs will avoid magma blocks that are in their way, so magma would make a great defense for your build.

LAVA

This block is extremely hot and does fire damage to surrounding blocks in the game. It also gives off a nice orange glow and can flow like water. Lava does a lot of damage to any player unlucky enough to touch it, so be careful!

LANTERN

These handy lights can be used to brighten things up at night or in shadowy areas. They have a light value higher than torches and can even melt snow within two blocks and ice within three. They can be placed on or hung from most other blocks.

《 BLOCK-I-PEDIA 》

TNT

Most fun block ever? Or the best way to clear large amounts of blocks at once? TNT blocks can be activated in many ways, including being set on fire or being close enough to other explosions. Also used in a variety of traps, this is one cool block!

BLAST FURNACE

Blast furnaces are mined using a pickaxe. They can be found in a village armorer and are used to smelt ores, armor, and tools. They can use different fuel types, such as blocks of coal, to run or give off light.

COMMAND BLOCK

Command blocks cannot be used in Survival mode (without cheats!) but are a tool that can be used in making custom maps in Creative mode. They can be made to do many things, including giving items to players. They are activated by redstone power.

GLOWSTONE

Glowstone only occurs naturally in the Nether, appearing on the underside of the netherrack. They glow with the brightest possible light in the game and can be used to make dark areas lighter. Mining with a tool enchanted with silk touch will make it drop itself.

PISTON

A piston is a handy type of block that can be used to push items or players. If you want to pull something instead, you can use a sticky piston, which is made by crafting a piston with a slimeball.

TOP TIP!

Minecraft masters like to use a particularly important block—redstone. Any build that has moving parts will need redstone to get things going!

≪ BLOCK-I-PEDIA ≫

STAINED GLASS

Stained glass is made by adding dye to a glass block. As they are colorful and see-through, you can have lots of fun decorating your buildings and creating different patterns.

16 colors to choose from

SHULKER BOX

A shulker box is a special type of storage that can be carried around and it protects its contents if broken. It can be dyed any of 16 colors and can also be undyed by using a cauldron. You can mine it with any tool or by hand.

SPONGE

This sponge block acts just like a real-life sponge and will soak up water with ease. Each block can absorb 65 water blocks. Once it has soaked up enough water it will become a wet sponge, which can be dried in a furnace.

PRISMARINE

This block appears as the main one that makes up an ocean monument. They are a strong block and great at standing up to explosions. They also glow in a cycle of different colors, so make excellent decoration.

《 BLOCK-I-PEDIA 》

BONE

Bone blocks can be mined using any pickaxe and can be found naturally underground as part of fossils. It seems as if they were left behind by creatures that have long since gone. They can be found in desert and swamp areas.

DIORITE

This block is a common type of igneous rock that can be mined using any pickaxe. It is most likely to be found on the surface of mountains. Diorite has the same blast resistance as stone, so can be used instead when building.

MUSHROOM

Mushroom blocks are what make up huge mushrooms. When broken apart with an axe, they drop three types of mushroom block—red mushroom blocks, brown mushroom blocks, and mushroom stems. These blocks can be used as fuel or composted.

GLASS PANEL

Glass is a very delicate material and can be very easily broken. That's why it requires a tool enchanted with silk touch to obtain. Glass panes are more efficient than glass blocks, so can be used to build much bigger windows.

TOP TIP!

Different colored glass blocks can really give your build the edge. Plus, they will give your city structures a super-modern vibe.

⟪ BLOCK-I-PEDIA ⟫

BUBBLE COLUMN

A bubble column is created when a magma block or soul sand is placed underwater. The column has the ability to move players in the direction of its flow. Bubble columns can be used by players to refill their air supply, making them useful for underwater-themed areas.

CAMP FIRE

A camp fire is made by crafting sticks, coal, and some kind of wood together. They are a useful block as they can be used to cook food, send a smoke signal, or as a light source. To make a camp fire into a signal fire you need to place a bale of hay beneath it.

COBWEB

Cobwebs can be obtained by using a pair of shears or a sword with a silk touch enchantment. Their main use is to slow down enemies, but they have no effect on spiders. This slowing effect will increase if the cobweb is placed on ice.

CORAL

Corals are non-solid blocks that come in five variants: tube, brain, bubble, fire, and horn. Coral likes to grow in warm oceans and will become dead coral if placed anywhere outside of water. As it is so colorful, coral makes a great addition to any ocean scene.

⟪ BLOCK-I-PEDIA ⟫

TORCH

Torches are a simple, but effective light source. They can be crafted with various chemicals to create different colors, or crafted into lanterns, jack o'lanterns, and even underwater torches. Very handy for exploring undersea passages!

OBSIDIAN

Obsidian is formed when flowing water hits a lava source block, and can be found naturally where water from a spring or lake has flowed over a nearby lava pool. It can only be mined using a diamond pickaxe. It's super strong against explosives.

FLOWER POT

A flower pot is a decorative block that can contain flowers, saplings, mushrooms, or plants. Flower pots naturally generate in witch huts (where they contain a red mushroom), the basement of igloos (where they contain a cactus), and woodland mansions.

WOOL

Wool is a classic Minecraft material that has been in the game for a decade. The fastest way to get wool is to shear a sheep, but it can be obtained without a tool as well. Wool can be dyed any of the 16 colors in the game and looks super soft and fluffy!

《 BLOCK-I-PEDIA 》

CARPET

Carpet can be mined using any tool, or even no tool, and can be crafted into a range of colors using different dyes. It is an amazing way to decorate the homes you build or to add details to large builds. Why not experiment with different patterns?

WATER

Even though it's officially a block, you can't pick up water unless you've got a bucket. It also behaves differently from other blocks—it spreads downward and may even affect other blocks it touches.

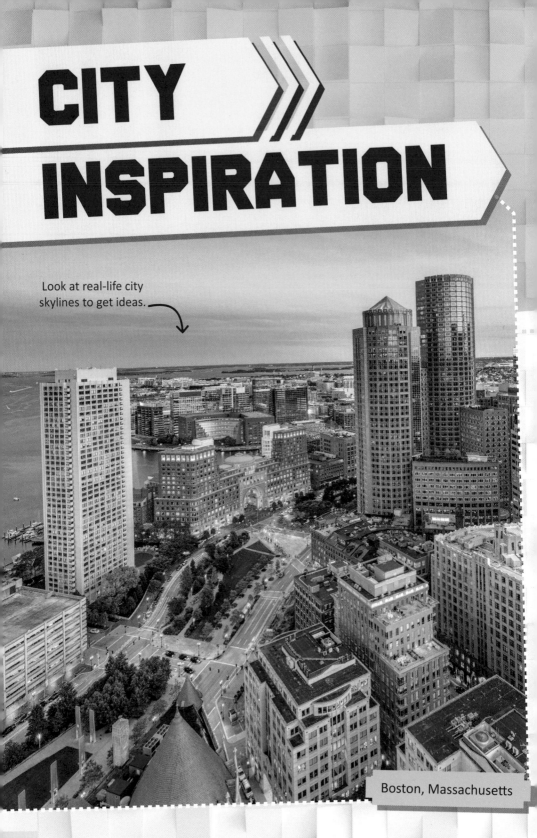

CITY >> INSPIRATION

Look at real-life city skylines to get ideas.

Boston, Massachusetts

Look at your builds from all angles—and don't forget the tops of the roofs!

Courtesy of MattuFin

GOOD IDEA

You could add a rooftop pool or sky garden to your tallest buildings for added cool!

Have a look online to get ideas for your city. See how real cities build up slowly over time, from smaller, older buildings made of stone and brick, to skyscraping modern towers made from glass and metal.

Cities built on a grid are easiest to replicate in Minecraft. Anywhere with old winding roads is harder to reproduce, but that doesn't mean you should avoid old-style builds. You have a wide range of materials available to you, so you can always pop an ancient temple alongside modernist masterpieces. And don't be limited by the builds in this book—you can add shops, galleries, and so much more.

Look to cities in the Middle East or key financial centers around the world for plenty of tall builds, but you might also feel inspired by your own hometown. No two cities are identical, and no two Minecraft cities are the same, so take your ideas from wherever you want to!

Why not replicate a famous landmark like the Seattle Space Needle?

Dubai, United Arab Emirates

Finish your skyscrapers with a point to make them as tall as possible.

=NM-CORP

Courtesy of spark-squared.com

WELCOME TO THE CITY

Now it's time to show you how to map out and build an amazing cityscape with a sports stadium, shops, housing, a skyscraper, and a subway. A real city is huge. We'll start small, but you can keep expanding your city until it's as big as you like.

≪ TAKE A LOOK ≫

This is the section of the city we're going to show you how to build. How you develop it after that is entirely up to you.

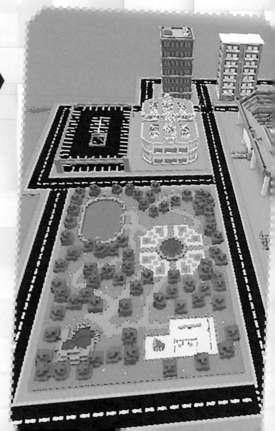

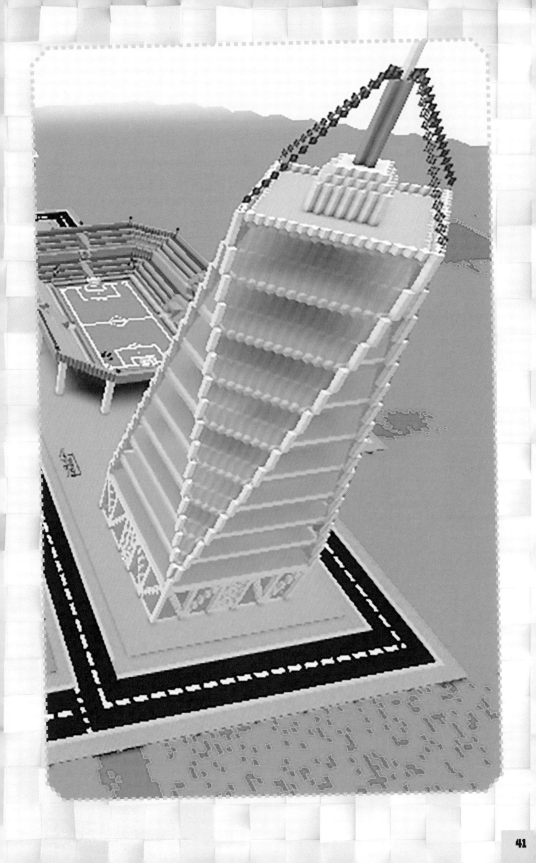

HERE'S HOW IT LOOKS FROM ABOVE

You can make the builds in any order you like. As long as you stick to the plan on page 51 and you make the paved areas and roads that help you put things in the right place, your city will fit together perfectly. There is unlimited space outside to expand it!

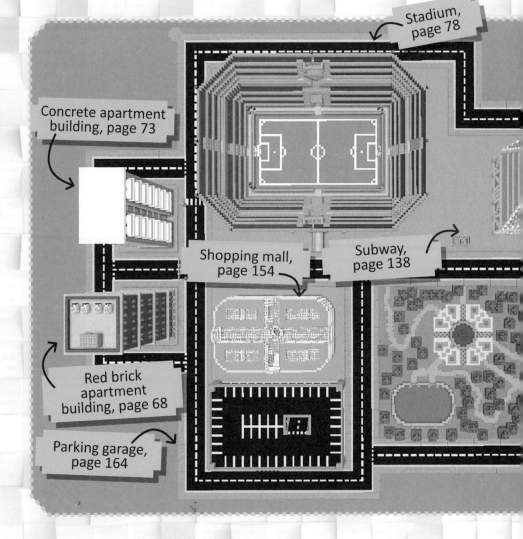

Stadium, page 78

Concrete apartment building, page 73

Shopping mall, page 154

Subway, page 138

Red brick apartment building, page 68

Parking garage, page 164

Use WorldEdit to copy and paste buildings to create a whole city.

Skyscraper, page 102

Park, page 172

《 CITYSCAPE 》

You don't have to make your city look just like this one. Feel free to use different colors and materials. As long as you stick to the basic structure and dimensions so that it all fits and works in the space, you can change the decorations. Your skyscraper could be a surreal construction of lapis lazuli and cobwebs. Your park could be a fantasy land of mushrooms and cacti with a lake of lava. Your road system need not be boring old black and white—it can be any colors you want!

GETTING CREATIVE

If you've only used Minecraft in Survival mode before, you'll be used to having to collect building materials and tools and avoiding all kinds of perils to stay alive. Building is a matter of survival and you might have settled for a hut to protect you. If you want to focus on building super structures, you can make life much easier for yourself by working in Creative mode. There will be no hostile mobs out to get you, and you'll have endless supplies of all the materials you want.

Superflat world

IT'S A FLAT, FLAT WORLD

It's pretty hard to build a city in the mountains or underwater. Luckily, Minecraft lets you choose a perfectly flat world for building so you don't have to struggle with the wrong type of landscape. Here's how to do it:

STEP 1

At the Select World screen, choose Create New World.

STEP 2

Give your new world a name, then click on the Game Mode button twice until it shows Game Mode: Creative.

STEP 3

Click on the button More World Options.

STEP 4

Click on the World Type button to show the option World Type: Superflat.

STEP 5

Click Done, and then Create New World. Your new world will start with unending views of green grass beneath a blue sky. Time to get building!

Courtesy of IAmNewAsWell

CHOOSING MATERIALS

In Creative mode, you don't need to hunt for materials or dig them out of the ground. They are available all the time. Press the E key to bring up the Building Blocks menu. You can pick up to nine materials to have immediately on hand and there's no limit to the number of blocks you can use.

GOOD FOUNDATIONS

In real life, buildings aren't plunked down directly on top of the ground—they would fall down. They have foundations underground to keep them solid and stable. In a real city, the structures would have poles and pillars going deep into the ground so that they would not fall or blow over and cause accidents. In Minecraft, we don't need to worry about foundations.

GROUND WORK

This plan shows the areas set aside for the different builds. As long as you follow it carefully, your city will come together perfectly. You'll also find a more detailed plan at the start of each build.

« ONE STEP AT A TIME »

The area on the ground that is occupied by a build is called its footprint.

Your subway goes underneath the city. The only part of it that shows on the plan is its entrance.

《 PERIMETER 》

The perimeter is the total distance around a shape. The city is not a rectangle. If you want to work out its perimeter, you have to add up the total length of all its sides:

107 + 42 + 57 + 150 + 32 + 60 + 179 + 113 + 14 + 97 + 61 + 42 = 954 blocks.

The perimeter is a line, so it has one dimension.

A

B

C

D

The area of a shape is the space it covers. To work out the area of the whole city, we would need to break it down into rectangles, work out the area of each rectangle, and add them all up:

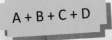

A + B + C + D

Area has two dimensions, so it's usually reported in square units, such as square feet (ft^2) or square miles (mi^2).

CITY PLANS

Orange and blue labels show the number of blocks used.

internal   external

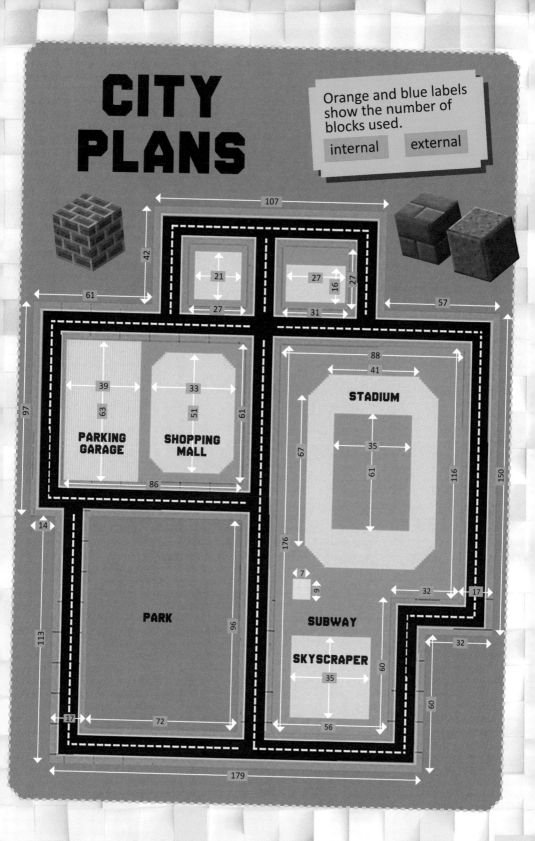

PARKING GARAGE

SHOPPING MALL

STADIUM

PARK

SUBWAY

SKYSCRAPER

107
42
61
21
27
27
16
27
31
57
39
33
88
41
63
51
61
97
86
35
67
61
116
150
14
176
113
96
7
9
32
17
17
60
35
60
32
60
17
72
56
179

PAVING THE WAY

Transportation and nature are both really important. In cities, keeping a good balance between roads and green spaces is never easy.

≪ ROAD CONSTRUCTION ≫

The road in your Minecraft city is concrete laid over clay in a trench. Real roads are also built from layers.

Work starts by digging a trench and making the bottom absolutely flat. Then construction workers dump layers of gravel (small, sharp stones) into the trench and compress it. The top layer is often asphalt, or sometimes concrete. Asphalt is a sticky, oil-based substance called bitumen mixed with sand and bits of rock. It's heated to 300 °F (150 °C) and spread over the gravel layers, then squashed and rolled flat before it cools and hardens. Asphalt is a bit flexible, so the road is unlikely to crack. It softens slightly in the heat, creating the sharp smell you sometimes get on hot summer roads.

A construction worker laying the asphalt layer of a road.

poppy

tall grass

CITIES AND GREEN SPACE

tree

Modern city planners try to make sure that people and wildlife have some green space, even in cities. Our city has a nice big park. But if you make your city larger, remember to leave extra green areas: sport fields, country parks, public gardens, or even a wild woodland area.

People who live in cities are healthier if they can get out for some fresh air and enjoy nature. In some countries, cities have a green belt (an area of land that can't be built on) to make sure the city-dwellers can easily get to a natural area.

sunflower

MATERIALS

STEP 1

Begin by marking out the perimeter of the city, using the dimensions in the plan to help you. The dark gray paving around the perimeter is three blocks wide and made from cobblestone slabs and stone brick slabs in a wavy pattern. The inside edge (or the curb) is made from stone slabs.

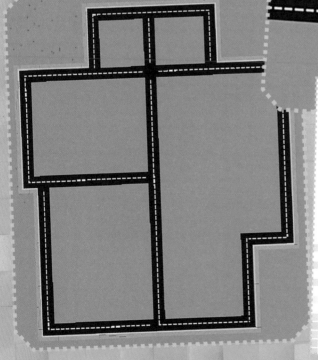

STEP 2

Now use the plan to help you lay the roads. Replace grass blocks with black and white concrete so that your roads are lower than your curbs. Build each road nine blocks wide with dashed white lines down the center. Each white stripe should be three blocks long with one black block on either side of it.

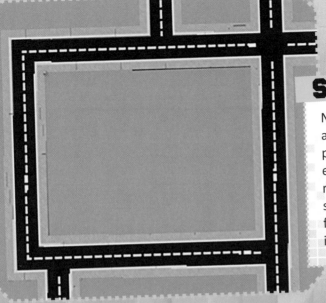

STEP 3

Next, add a curb and dark gray paving along the edges of all of your roads, just the same as you did for the perimeter in Step 1.

STEP 4

Use stone blocks to cover the rest of the grass inside the perimeter, except for in the park.

TRANSPORTATION SYSTEM

A lot of planning goes into roads, from their angles and curves to how the traffic moves along them in the most efficient way. Nobody likes a traffic jam!

≪ BEST BENDS ≫

Real roads don't have corners like right angles. Vehicles could not deal with roads like this. Instead, real roads have rounded corners or slow bends.

To make a curved corner, a road engineer has to start curving the road some way back from where the right angle would fall. The farther back the curve starts, the gentler it will be. You can think of the curve as being part of a circle. The distance from the center of a circle to the edge is called the radius. The larger the radius of the circle, the gentler the curve will be, and the safer it will be to drive around.

《 STOP, WAIT, GO! 》

An **intersection** is where roads join one another, giving people a choice of routes. To bring traffic together safely and keep it moving, intersections often use traffic lights or traffic circles to let vehicles take turns.

At **traffic lights**, vehicles stop at a red light and wait for a green light before entering an intersection.

The lights are set up so that traffic from one direction at a time can go, keeping everyone safe.

At a **traffic circle**, vehicles stop or slow down as they come up to a circle of road. They can only drive into the circle if there is no traffic on it already coming toward them. Drivers wait until it's safe, and go round to the exit they want.

An engineer's sketch of a curve in the road.

STEP 5

Add the three-way intersection markings. Across the roads where drivers have to yield, add a dotted line made from alternating blocks of white and black concrete. The traffic going in a straight line (not having to turn a corner) generally has right of way. Don't forget the entrance to the parking garage.

STEP 6

Create a four-way intersection with traffic lights between the apartment buildings, the shopping mall, and the stadium so the traffic can take turns at moving and not get jammed. Add dotted lines across the end of each of the four roads to form a square where they meet. Knock out a paving slab at each corner and build a column from cobblestone wall seven blocks tall. Join them along the top, using more cobblestone wall. Add two traffic lights on each side, two blocks in from each end, with a gap of three blocks between them. Each traffic light is made of three polished andesite blocks with item frames attached to the front of them, containing red, yellow, and lime concrete blocks.

TOP TIP!

Where roads meet each other, you need to mark the intersection so that drivers know whether they are allowed to go straight on or whether they have to yield to traffic coming from another direction.

STEP 7

Finally, add a crosswalk so that people can cross the road safely. Lay white concrete stripes into the road, one block wide and three blocks long, lined up with one of the center lines in the road. Then add traffic lights on cobblestone wall columns on each side of the road.

HIGH-RISE HOUSING

HIGH-RISE LIVING
INSPIRATION

A city is full of people, and people need somewhere to live. Let's start by building a couple of high-rise apartment buildings for them. A whole city will need lots more housing, but you can adapt or repeat these all over the city once you know how to create them.

Curved walls like these are harder to achieve in Minecraft, but you can easily use two similar colors for a subtle striped effect.

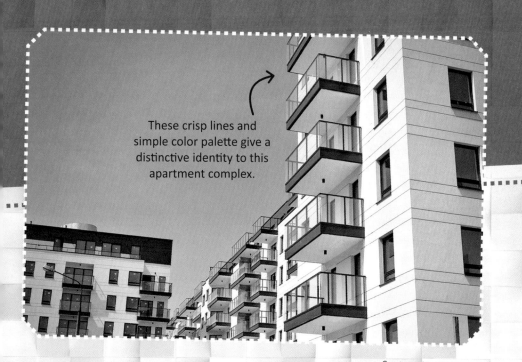

These crisp lines and simple color palette give a distinctive identity to this apartment complex.

Courtesy of Forbidden Coder

The best thing about apartment buildings in Minecraft is that all you need to do is design one floor and then duplicate it all the way to the top. You might then want to add a penthouse with extra room or facilities.

When designing high-rise living for your city, it's important not to forget the outside. Try to give each apartment a balcony or even give the whole building a stunning roof garden!

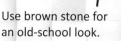

Use brown stone for an old-school look.

«LIVING ON THE BLOCK»

Here's the layout for the apartment buildings. Look carefully at the plan and refer back to it as you are building. It has all the dimensions you will need to use. The plan is shown to scale. Your build will have exactly the same proportions as the picture in the plan.

MATERIALS

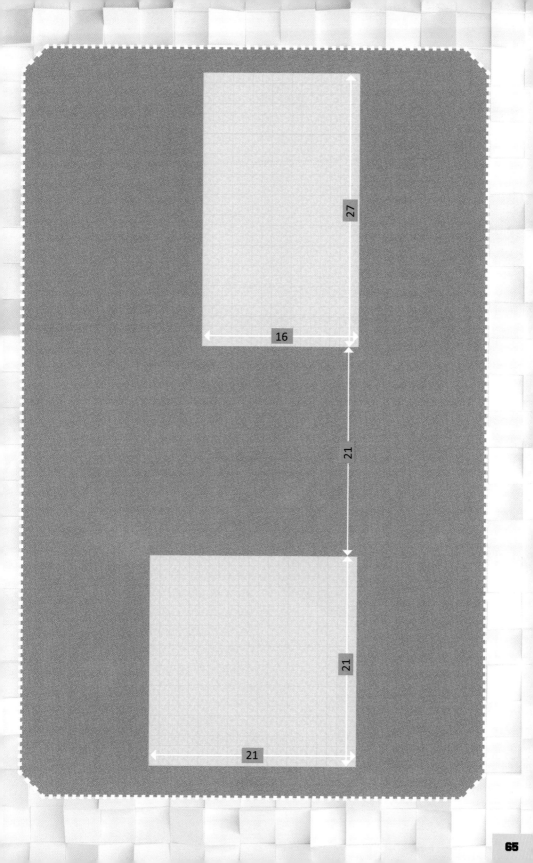

LIVING ROOM

In cities, many people live in high-rise apartment buildings as more people can fit into the same area of ground than if they live in houses. The materials that are used need to keep people safe as well as give them a good quality of life.

bricks

❰❰ SPACED OUT ❱❱

A house with an area of 10x20 blocks can house a family of four. An apartment building with an area of 20x20 blocks can house two families of four on each floor. So, an apartment building with six floors can house 48 people. To work out how many families can live in a building, calculate its volume

length x width x height

stone block

and divide this by the space needed to house each family.

≪ TALL ORDER ≫

Most buildings are made of bricks, stone, or concrete as these are hard materials that stand up to extreme weather and last a long time. You don't want buildings to fall down in a high wind or to dissolve in the rain! It's important to choose materials with the properties important for the purpose; bricks, stone, and granite are ideal for your first apartment building.

white concrete

Tall buildings, like this skyscraper, save a lot of space on the ground and can accommodate thousands of people.

STEP 1

Refer to the plan for the whole city so you start in the right place. In the center of the 27x27 paved area where your red brick block of flats is going to go, build a 21x21 square outline for the outside walls. Leave an opening for the door in the middle of the front wall, then build the walls five blocks high leaving space for the windows in each side.

STEP 2

Add stone brick stairs in front of the wall, but use stone slabs in front of each window. Don't block the door!

STEP 3

Before you build the next story, add a layer of polished granite to the top of the brick. Then build up the window pillars to match the ground floor. Above the front door, add another window instead of a door.

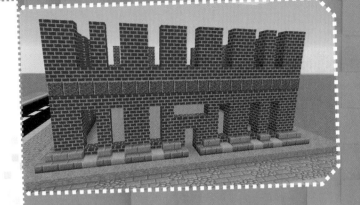

STEP 4

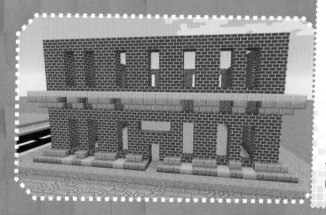

Place upside-down stone brick stairs on the outside of the granite, but leave a space above the windows. Then add a layer of stone slabs on top of the stairs all around the building to make a ledge.

STEP 5

Add another row of polished granite slabs all around the top of the wall, and continue the brickwork to make a third story. You can repeat this step as many times as you like to make your apartment building as tall as you want it to be.

WHAT A SIGHT!

If we live in a place that looks nice, we feel happy. You could say, the things we surround ourselves with are pretty important! Even in nature, symmetry is a sign of beauty.

« CLEAR VIEW »

Glass is translucent, which means it lets light through. Just what you need for windows! Materials that don't let light through are opaque—like the walls of this building.

bookshelf

painting

glass block

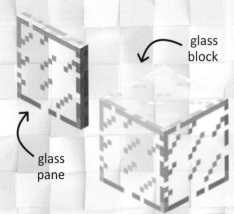

glass pane

« INTERIORS »

In a real apartment block, there would be internal walls and doors, stairs between the floors, and an elevator shaft. You could add these inside your apartment building if you like. Builders make important structural walls while they are building the outside, but add doors, stairs, and internal walls afterward. You could even decorate the rooms with paintings, bookshelves, and furniture when you have finished.

SYMMETRY

A symmetrical shape is one that has matching halves. It can be folded in half exactly so that one half covers the other. The letter "E" is symmetrical from top to bottom; fold it in half horizontally and the shape of both halves is the same. The letter "A" is symmetrical from left to right; fold it vertically and both sides match.

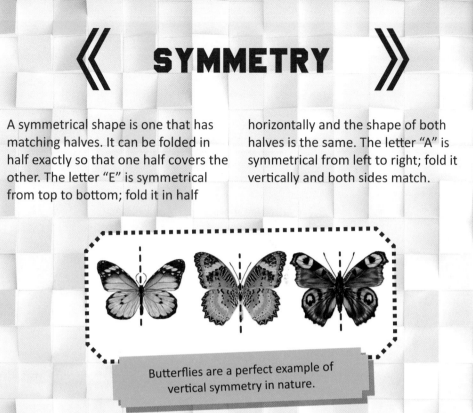

Butterflies are a perfect example of vertical symmetry in nature.

A square has left-right and up-down symmetry, and it also has diagonal symmetry. A rectangle has left-right and up-down symmetry, but does not have diagonal symmetry. Because it's square, the plan for the red brick apartment building has left-right, up-down, and diagonal symmetry.

The plan for the gray apartment building has left-right and up-down symmetry.

Symmetry is key in architecture as it creates balance and proportion. Most buildings are rectangular, as they are quicker, cheaper, and easier to build.

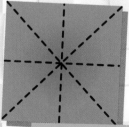

A square has four lines of symmetry, but a rectangle only has two.

STEP 6

Every second floor, add the decorative stone border again. Inside, add a floor of oak wood plank at the level of each row of granite blocks. Then add glass panes to all the windows.

STEP 7

Finally, add a roof made from stone slabs. On top of this add a 3x7 elevator box and four 2x3 air-conditioning units. The elevator is made of polished andesite with an iron door. The air-con units are made of iron blocks with iron bars in front, with a circle of curved rail, and a piece of powered rail on top.

STEP 8

Build the second apartment building just across the street from the first one. Dig a 27x16 rectangle two blocks deep in the 31x27 paved area. Leave a rim two blocks wide at the front and sides and seven blocks wide at the back. Line the floor with stone brick.

STEP 9

Start building the ground floor. There are a lot of windows in these apartments that we need to leave space for. Make the front and back walls and the top rows along the side walls from polished andesite. Use quartz blocks for the side walls and the top rows above the windows at the front and back. Lay oak wood plank flooring throughout.

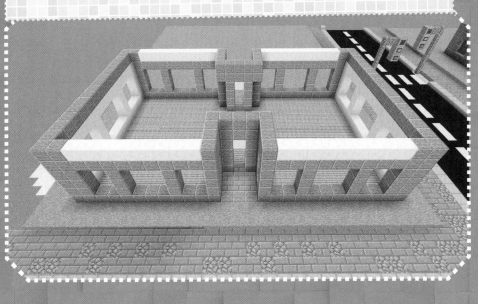

ROTATE AND TRANSLATE

Understanding how to copy and repeat shapes is vital in real-life construction as well as when you're building in Minecraft.

《 BACK TO FRONT 》

The front of the concrete apartment building is a mirror image of the back. If you put a mirror across the middle of the building, from left to right, the reflection in the mirror looks exactly the same as the back of the building.

When an object is reflected, its left-hand side appears on the right, and its right-hand side appears on the left (or its top appears at the bottom and its bottom at the top). The reflection is the same distance from the mirror line as the object.

Symmetrical shape | Reflection

Asymmetrical shape | Reflection

《 DO YOU COPY? 》

Reflection is one type of transformation. Other types are translation and rotation.

A translated shape is exactly the same as the original, but moved to a different place. It is not rotated, resized or reflected.

These apartment buildings, facing the same direction, but in different places, are an example of translation.

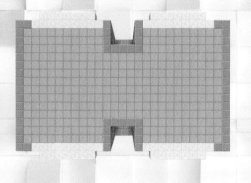

A rotated object is turned around. It is not changed or moved in any other way.

These apartment blocks, facing in different directions, are an example of rotation.

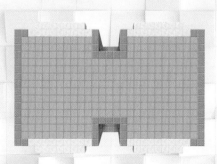

STEP 10

Now we'll add the next floor. Begin by creating a floor of stone slabs, with a single row of quartz front and back. Then add an overhanging row of quartz, two blocks shorter, above the windows front and back. These will then form the balconies in the finished building.

STEP 11

Next, build up the walls for this story using polished andesite and stone brick. They are one block in from the walls below.

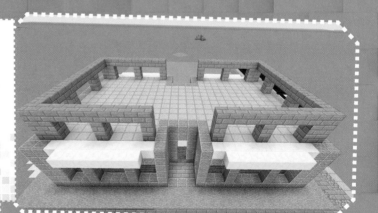

The people who live in these apartments will enjoy sitting on their balconies watching the city. Put a row of quartz slabs around the quartz blocks and add glass panes to the slabs. These will stop people falling off the balconies, but they will still be able to see through them.

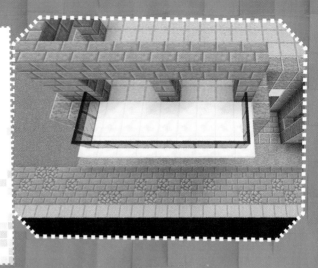

STEP 13

Add a layer of polished andesite blocks all around the outside walls (but not the balcony columns) to make the walls flush with those on the ground floor. Then create balconies using black stained glass panes.

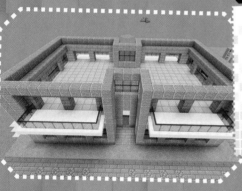

STEP 14

Repeat Steps 10–13 to add as many more floors as you want. When you've finished, use quartz blocks to make the roof.

STADIUM

Large shared spaces bring people together and build community spirit. The people of the city would love to watch some sport events. So let's make a stadium!

STADIUM INSPIRATION

Courtesy of KsdKak12

If you're a sports fan, this research is going to be right in your ballpark! Pick your favorite team and look at their home ground, or find your inspiration from one of the big national sports locations.

You will need to think about what sport or sports you want played in your stadium—make sure the markings are right! And it's important to squeeze as many spectators as possible into your

San Siro,
Milan, Italy

build to make sure when the crowd goes wild, they will really raise the roof (if your stadium has one!).

You might also want to think about how your stadium could work as a music venue—where would the stage go? And are there screens at either end for close ups?

Parking lots, restrooms, and refreshment stands are all things that you will need to bear in mind when planning a stadium, not to mention the merch stand!

TOP TIP!

Think about the weather—make sure the spectators will be shaded from the sun and also kept dry if it rains. Make your roof slope out rather than in, like a funnel!

MATERIALS

TOP TIP!

This is a soccer field. If you'd like to watch a different game, use WORKING WITH SCALE on page 85 to help you work out the new dimensions you will need.

17

41

35

17

61

16

67

《 A FIELD DAY 》

Here's the plan for the stadium. It has a soccer field in the middle and stands for spectators all around the sides. Refer back to the plan as you build, making sure you get all the dimensions right for the tunnels, stands, and commentators' boxes. You can make the stadium slightly wider or narrower if you want to have a different type of playing field, but try to keep the length about the same.

penalty box

penalty arc

goal box

STEP 1

Using the city plan as a guide, build a 35x61 rectangle of grass block on top of your stone paving. Mark out a 31x57 rectangle on top of it with white wool. Divide it down the middle and add a circle with a diameter of seven blocks in the center. Make 5x9 goal boxes, 11x17 penalty boxes and 3x5 penalty arcs. Build two goals, each five blocks wide and three blocks tall, from iron block with cobweb nets.

TAKING SHAPE

Understanding shapes and sizes is essential when you're building.

 ## CIRCLES AND LINES

The perimeter of a circle is called its circumference. The line drawn through the center of a circle to the circumference is its diameter. The diameter is the same length wherever you draw it. The diameter always cuts the circle in half. A line from the edge of a circle to the middle is called the radius, and is half the diameter.

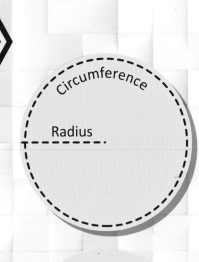

Circumference

Radius

Diameter

⟪ WORKING WITH SCALE ⟫

If you want to use your stadium for a different game, you'll need to change the markings and possibly the size. Try to keep the length about the same, so that it still fits inside its footprint in your plan of the city.

A doubles tennis court is 36 ft (11 m) x 78 ft (24 m).

An easy scale to use would be 1 ft: 1 block.

However, if you want a smaller court, you could experiment with scaling it to 1.5 or 2 blocks for each foot.

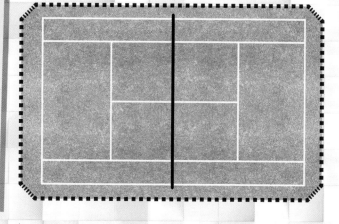

Your soccer field takes up an area of 35x61.

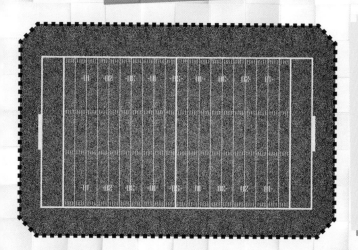

A football field is about 53 yards (49 m) x 100 yards (92 m).

If you halve 53, you get 26.5, and if you halve 100, you get 50.

A good scale to use could be 1 yard: 0.5 blocks.

STEP 2

Around the perimeter of the 35x61x1 grass rectangle, add a row of stone brick two blocks high. Then, add a row of stone, a row of double stone slabs, and another row of stone slabs all one block high.

STEP 3

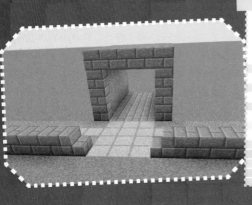

Opposite the center line halfway down the field, remove seven blocks from the wall and add stone brick stair either side of the gap. Replace 3x4 of the path with double stone slabs. Replace 3x7 grass blocks with stone bricks to create a path. Then build a 5x4 tunnel over the path from stone brick and stone.

glass safety barrier

STEP 4

Now build the stands. On each side of the tunnel, add diagonal rows of stone brick stairs. Make these four blocks long and five blocks high. Either side of the stairs, make the stands from polished andesite. Each layer is two blocks deep and two blocks high. Add light gray stained glass panes along the front of each stand as a safety barrier.

Extend the top of the stairs using stone brick to make a platform that is five blocks deep. Build two sets of steps up from the middle of the platform. Make them three blocks wide and four blocks high. At the top of each set of stairs, build a walkway from stone and double stone slab. Extend it to the end of the stands.

STEP 6

Fill in the wall between the new path and the stand below. Add gray stained glass along the front edge of the path. Then build another two sets of stairs, three blocks wide and five blocks high, with a row of stone brick between them.

CAN THEY SEE?

The seats in the stadium are tiered; they are higher up further from the sports field and lower down nearer the field. This means people at the back still have a good view. They need clear sight lines to see the game, without the heads of people in front blocking their view.

An example of blocked sight lines.

An example of clear sight lines.

≪ ANGLES AND TRIANGLES ≫

We could have built a rectangular stadium, but this wouldn't have given customers in the corners a very good view because they would have had to turn at an angle to see the field. We won't fit quite as many spectators in with the arrangement we've chosen, but at least they won't grumble!

A right-angled triangle has one angle of 90 degrees.

We removed the shape of a right-angled triangle from the four corners of the stadium.

You can work out the length of the long side (called the hypotenuse) if you know the lengths of the other two sides.

$(a \times a) + (b \times b) = (c \times c)$

This can be written as:

$$a^2 + b^2 = c^2$$

In our triangles, a and b are the same length.

The commentator's box will fit in the gap between the staircases. Make it 9x4x4, using stone with polished andesite at the front. Use oak wood stairs for the commentators' chairs and give them microphones made of iron bars. Cover the front with gray stained glass panes; it cuts glare and gives the commentators a good view of the field.

STEP 8

Make stands for this second tier, the same as on the lower level, on either side of the stairs.

STEP 9

On the opposite side of the stadium, repeat Steps 3–8 so the stands look exactly the same.

STEP 10

Now make the stands at the ends of the field, behind the goals. Add a staircase in the middle, five blocks wide and five blocks high, with stands of the same design as the others.

STEP 11

glass safety barrier

At the back of the last stand, build a wall four blocks high and three blocks deep using stone and double stone slabs. Add ladders above the steps and finish with a safety barrier made from gray stained glass panes.

STEP 12

Then starting from the landing behind the ladders, add another staircase, five blocks wide and five blocks high. Build stands on either side of this, as before.

SAFE AND SOUND

The support structure is one of the most important features of a real building, but something you'll never have to worry about in Minecraft. Lighting, on the other hand, is vital in both places.

≪ SUPPORTING A BUILDING ≫

You couldn't build a real stadium in the sequence you are building your Minecraft one. The stands would not be at all stable unless supports were added at the start. A stadium like this would have much more support, with supporting walls beneath the tiers of the stands.

Some columns go deep into the ground while others support the building above ground level.

Horizontal support structures give columns extra strength.

AUTOMATIC LIGHTING

Lights that turn on automatically when it starts to get dark respond to the amount of light falling on a sensor. Often, people have garden or patio lights that come on in the evening. Motion sensors are also often used with lights. These respond to movement nearby to turn on a security light. In both cases, a sensor picks up a stimulus (falling light levels, or movement) and triggers a switch in an electric circuit.

When the light level falls, the sensor outside this house triggers a switch to turn on the lights.

daylight sensor

STEP 13

Your stadium now has four sides, but there are big gaps in the corners! Fill these in by adding one extra block to the back row of each stand and then laying blocks, corner-to-corner, across the gap to join up the stands at each level.

STEP 14

Fill in the gaps to extend the stands around the corner. Don't forget to add the safety barrier! The stands and the safety barrier will have a zig-zag pattern. Add a wall two blocks high behind the highest stand—we don't want anyone to fall off.

STEP 15

We're going to keep supporters of the competing teams separate. To make sure everyone knows where to go, color-code the two halves of the stadium by laying carpet on the stands.

STEP 16

This stadium is hanging in mid-air at the moment, and that's not very safe. Add two 2x2x14 iron block supports at each corner and in the middle of each side.

STEP 17

Build hollow 5x4x3 ticket booths at the ends of the entrance tunnels from Step 3. Use polished andesite, iron bar, and signs. Add turnstiles made from iron bar and fence. Add a path to the pavement using oak fence, stone slabs, and stone brick.

STEP 18

Finally, in each corner of the field and in the top corners of the stands, add lighting made from redstone lamps, daylight sensors, and fence. Right-click the daylight sensor to set your lights to turn on at night.

SKYSCRAPER

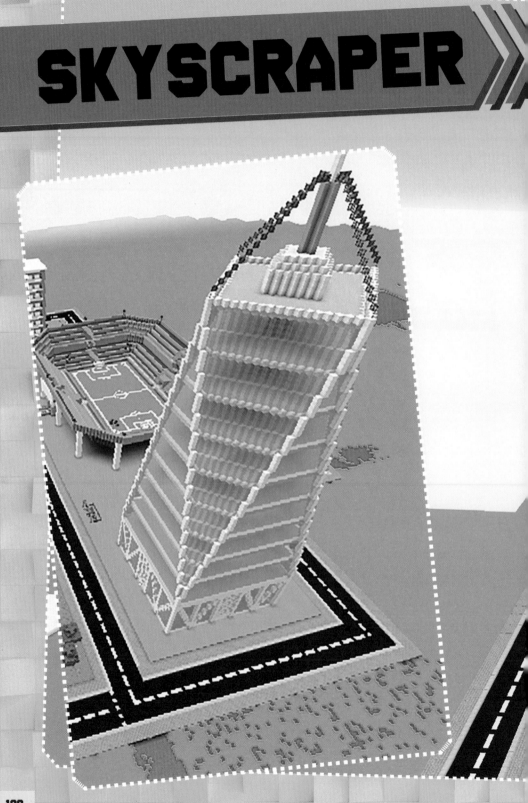

SKYSCRAPER INSPIRATION

Modern cities are famous for their skyscrapers. They even compete with each other for the biggest, most dramatic, and most bizarre designs. Most new skyscrapers are spectacular constructions of glass and steel—and that's what you're going to add to your city now.

Modern skyscrapers come in all shapes and sizes, but they are all very tall!

Like the apartment blocks, skyscrapers can be built quite quickly in Minecraft by duplicating floors.

When planning your skyscraper, you will need to think about the various functions your build will need to fulfill. Most skyscrapers are predominantly work places, but they can also house shops at the bottom and a restaurant at the top. You might also want to include a gym and residential space.

But the most important thing to consider is the architectural impact. Look at skyscrapers from around the world to see just how different their visual impact can be.

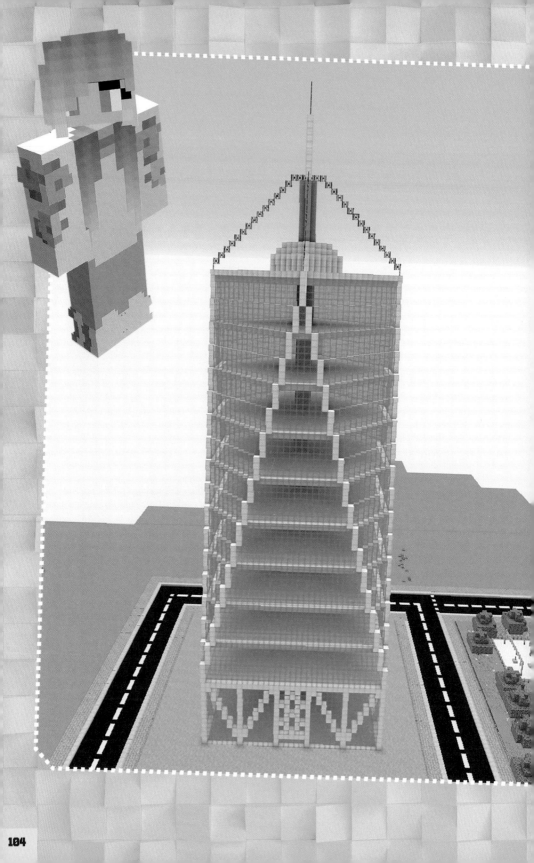

⟪ PERFECT PLACE ⟫

The skyscraper is across the road from the park. This means workers can go for a walk outside during their lunch break. It's right next to the entrance to the subway so that people can easily get to and from work.

The Shard, London

The Burj Khalifa, Dubai

MATERIALS

A skyscraper can accommodate many workers within a small area because it stretches up toward the sky.

The viewing platform at the top of a skyscraper is a great way to see the layout of a city.

35

35

« WHAT'S INSIDE? »

Most skyscrapers contain offices where people work. Some are occupied by just one large organization, such as a bank or a government department. Others are divided up so several different organizations share the building.

Although lots of space is used for offices, there is usually room for coffee shops, restaurants, and perhaps even a gym for the people who work there. Some skyscrapers have shops at the bottom. A few have restaurants or viewing platforms at the very top, giving spectacular views over the city.

STRONG STRUCTURES

You don't need foundations or strong shapes for your Minecraft builds, but in the real world they are essential.

≪ FIRM FOUNDATIONS ≫

Constant vibrations from heavy traffic and subways plus high winds and even earthquakes threaten the stability of skyscrapers, so they need solid foundations. The foundations for a house might consist of a pit filled with rubble, but for a skyscraper the builders might dig all the way down to rock to provide a solid base. They might drive long, thick metal columns, called piles, deep into the ground to support the structure.

Once the piles have been driven deep into the ground, builders can lay the building's foundations.

THE MIGHTY TRIANGLE

Some shapes are stronger or more stable than others. If you push on one side of a rectangle, it's quite easy to bend it out of shape. The angles between its sides can change, turning it into a parallelogram. The structure can fail even though the sides don't come apart.

Force

→

Triangles aren't easily distorted like this. Pushing on one side of a triangle doesn't alter the angles.

Force

→

Triangles are strong shapes that are difficult to distort. When creating a building in the real world, architects and engineers have to think about the kinds of pressures and stresses that could damage the building. Diagonal struts are often used to turn large rectangles into triangles.

STEP 1

Using the city plan as a guide, mark out the 35x35 square base of the skyscraper, using iron blocks set into the ground. Start building in the large paved space next to the stadium.

TOP TIP!

Add a pattern to your floor as well as your walls. Use several of the 16 different colored hardened clays Minecraft has to offer to create a stunning modern mosaic.

STEP 2

Using iron blocks, build the frame for your first section. Make it 14 blocks high with columns in each corner. Build another four columns along each side, with a gap of five blocks between the two central columns and six between the rest. Add four diagonal struts between the columns on each wall to make V-shapes. Create a geometric pattern between the two central columns on each wall.

doorway

Fill in all the gaps with light blue stained glass blocks. Leave a central doorway two blocks tall in the middle of each side.

doorway

SUPPORT STRUCTURES

In Minecraft builds, no structural support is needed. A single layer of blocks can form the ceiling and the floor above it. Not so in real life...

≪ LONG AND STRONG ≫

Columns have been used to hold up parts of buildings for thousands of years. They can support a roof without the need for solid walls all the way round a building. Ancient Greek and Roman temples and other buildings had columns of special designs called Doric, Ionian, and Corinthian.

≪ ABOVE AND BELOW ≫

In a real building, the ceiling and floor are separate, with a space between. Joists are laid across the building between the walls. The ceiling is fastened to the lower surface of the joists, and the floor to the upper surface. Insulation placed in this gap helps to stop heat moving up through the building and also provides soundproofing between floors.

As well as insulation, there are electrical cables and water pipes in the space between the ceiling and the upper floor.

Doric

Ionian

Corinthian

A Doric column is wider at the bottom than at the top, and is the strongest type. It has no separate base. The other two types are the same width all the way up and stand on a base. Columns are still used in modern buildings, especially when there are no internal walls. You can often see them in large, open buildings like parking garages and airports.

STEP 4

Fill in the space between the iron blocks at the top with double stone slabs to make a ceiling and a floor.

STEP 5

Inside the building, add a light blue concrete pillar in the middle, going from the floor to the ceiling. Then build four cyan concrete pillars around it, one at each corner.

STEP 6

Three blocks out from the central pillar, make a reception desk from a 9x9 square made from cobblestone wall topped with stone slabs that goes all around the pillar.

STEP 7

Back outside, create the iron block frame for the next floor. Add a 4x1 column to each corner of the building. Then place two more 4x1 columns diagonally on top of each column. Placing the blocks diagonally like this is the first step toward creating triangle-shaped walls. Link the corner columns together with rows of blocks.

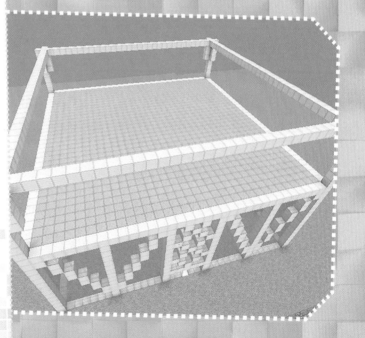

SHAPES AND STRUCTURES

Buildings contain many different shapes.
These shapes work together to give
each building its own look.

⟪ SKY-SHAPE-ER ⟫

❯ SQUARE

The base of the
skyscraper is a square.

- four equal sides
- four right (90 degree) angles

❯ RECTANGLE

If the skyscraper had
vertical sides, they
would be rectangular.

- sides of two
  different lengths
- four right
  (90 degree) angles

But as you build this skyscraper
higher, instead of vertical sides
you build diagonal sides.

❯ ISOSCELES TRIANGLE

Eventually the sides meet in a
point at the top to form isosceles
triangles, with two equal angles
and two equal sides.

- three sides
- angles that
  add up to 180
  degrees

≪ POLYGONS ≫

A multi-sided shape is called a polygon. Polygons can be regular or irregular. A square and an equilateral triangle are both regular polygons. A rectangle and an isosceles triangle are both examples of irregular polygons. An irregular polygon has some sides of unequal length, even if a few are equal.

As the diagonal sides of your skyscraper grow, the skyscraper's floor shape changes from a square to an irregular octagon. Halfway up, it will be a regular octagon, with eight equal sides. Then it will be an irregular octagon through the following floors until it's square again.

The below sequence shows the changing floor shape of your skyscraper.

long sides

long sides

STEP 8

Fill in the walls with light blue stained glass and add a ceiling made from double stone slabs.

STEP 9

Repeat Step 5 to create the pillar in the center of the floor.

STEP 10

Repeat Steps 7–9 to build the next floor. At the corners, place columns diagonally on top of the previous ones to make the triangle-shaped walls grow with each new floor.

STEP 11

Keep on adding more floors by repeating Steps 7–9. The upside down (inverted) triangles will get wider as the width of the adjacent sides reduces.

STEP 12

As you keep going, you will notice that the ceilings you are filling in are no longer square. You have cut the corners off the skyscraper making the inverted triangles, so the floors are becoming octagonal.

HIGH AND MIGHTY

The triangular sides of your skyscraper make it very strong and its towering walls of glass will always stay clean. But what do we do in the real world to make sure skyscrapers stay dirt-free?

《 SQUEAKY CLEAN 》

Most skyscrapers have a lot of glass, and that means they take a lot of cleaning! Windows get dirty from rain mixed with dust in the air, from bird droppings, and from pollution. It would soon be hard to see through the windows if they weren't cleaned.

Many are still cleaned by brave, expert window cleaners working from platforms or wires hundreds of feet above the ground. Others are cleaned by special machines. But some skyscrapers have self-cleaning glass. This has a special coating that reacts with sunlight to break down and loosen dirt. Then, when it rains, the rain spreads over the whole window like a sheet of water and washes away the loose dirt. No one needs to do anything!

THE BIG THREE

ISOSCELES

The triangles on the sides of your skyscraper are isosceles triangles. Isosceles triangles have two sides of the same length and one side of a different length. Two of their angles are the same, and one is different. They can be tall and thin, or short and squat.

EQUILATERAL

A triangle with all three sides the same length also has three angles the same. It's called an equilateral triangle.

RIGHT-ANGLED TRIANGLE

A triangle that has a right angle (90 degrees) is a right-angled triangle. If both the other angles are 45 degrees, it's also an isosceles triangle.

Workers clean the outside of a skyscraper.

Eventually, the sides will narrow into points and the corners will widen into long edges.

STEP 14

Keep repeating Steps 7–9 until each side reaches a point, the corners become the sides and the ceiling is square again!

top floor
overlapping
ground floor

TOP TIP!

You'll notice all the blocks are now lying diagonally. This is because the square roof has turned through 45 degrees and it doesn't line up with the square base.

STEP 15

People will need to go onto the roof, so we'd better make it safe. Build a wall one block tall all around the top edge, over the top of the blue glass blocks.

STEP 16

In the center of the roof, build a 7x7x4 cuboid using iron blocks. This is the base for the radio antennae.

HIDDEN POWERS

Skyscrapers are great places to send clear radio signals from. They are also more flexible than you might think—they can sway gently from side to side in the wind.

« WAVES IN SPACE »

Radio waves are waves of electromagnetic energy. Other types of electromagnetic waves include light, X-rays, and microwaves (the same as in a microwave oven). Radio waves can travel through air or space, but they can be stopped by some materials, such as the steel structure of a building.

radio waves

Radio antennae are often put on top of skyscrapers because they are taller than the other buildings around them. Up high there is very little to interfere with the radio waves.

⟪ BENDY BUILDINGS ⟫

The tops of some skyscrapers can move from side to side by up to a few feet in really strong winds. This isn't dangerous, in fact it makes the building safer because some movement in one part of the building stops the whole building feeling the full force of the wind. Many skyscrapers are now built with tuned mass dampers at the top. Tuned mass dampers stay still, like an anchor, while the rest of the building moves in response to wind or earth tremors. Their heavy suspended weight absorbs and balances the movement of the earth or the wind to help keep the building steady.

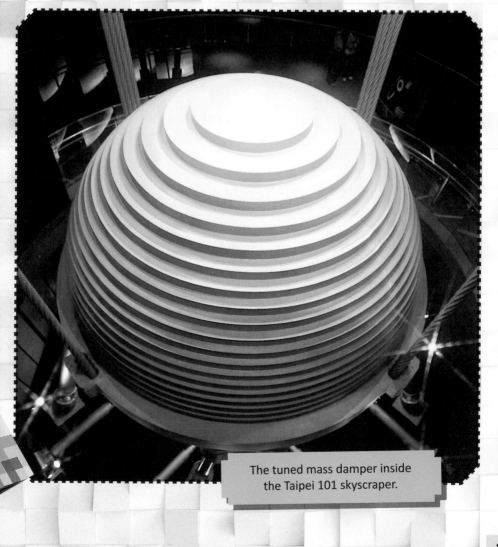

The tuned mass damper inside the Taipei 101 skyscraper.

One block in from the top edge of the base, add a 6x6 layer of blocks. On top of that add another layer, this time 5x5, to complete the roof.

STEP 18

In the middle of the roof, use five gray concrete blocks to make a cross-shape. Build this 10 blocks high to create the first section of your radio antenna.

STEP 19

Add a 10x1 column made from iron blocks to create the second section of the antennae.

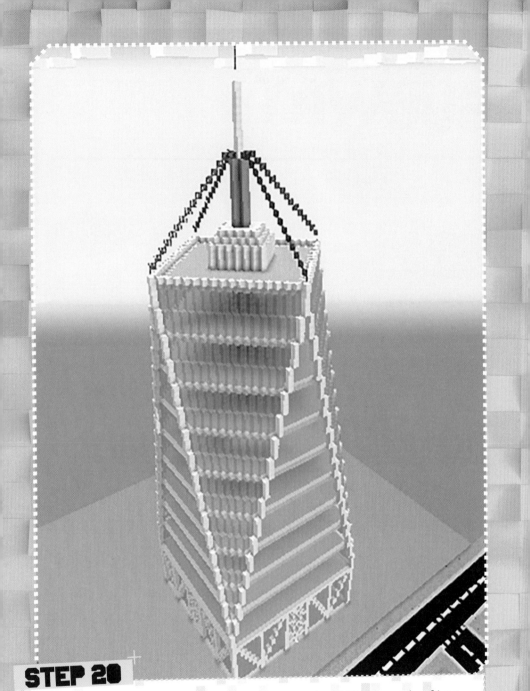

STEP 20

On top of the thinner column, add the antenna itself. This is made of iron bar and is five blocks tall. The antenna could still blow around and bend or break in high winds. Add strong cables to hold it in position through the fiercest storms. Use iron bar to connect the middle of the antenna support to the corners of the building to keep it secure and stable.

SUBWAY

SUBWAY INSPIRATION

Whether it's called the metro, the tube, or the underground, when somewhere has a large population, it's essential to have a way of quickly getting from one side of a city to the other. Some underground lines are now over 100 years old, but stations can be super modern.

In many ways a subway is an obvious build in Minecraft—after all you're used to tunneling through the ground in search of special blocks. Lighting is essential, so think about how the light works in the entrance to the station and exactly where to position lighting down on the platform.

TOP TIP!
Underground platforms can be quite dark, so make sure you mark the edges with yellow for safety.

Safety barriers and ways of getting down to the trains are a must.

Every large city needs a subway system so people can move around without clogging up the roads with traffic. We'll make a start on an underground train-line here—you can expand it as your city grows.

⟪ DOWN UNDER ⟫

Unlike the other builds, most of this is underground. All kinds of buildings go above subways. This is the plan for the subway station you will build. Remember that only the entrance will be visible above the ground.

UNDER THE CITY

People began building subway systems in the 1800s. The trains in those days were all coal-driven steam trains, so the tunnels were dirty, smoky, and smelly. Today, underground trains run on electric lines. They're cleaner, quieter, and safer. City planners work out where people want to go and engineers work out the best routes. Above ground, people can change direction and choose to go by different roads. Below ground, they can only stay on the train and go where the train goes, so it needs to go to the right places!

Start by building above the ground, making the entrance to the first station. We'll put it next to the sports stadium, as lots of people will want to go there.

MATERIALS

sign

TOP TIP!

Use signs to provide directions and also to give each of your stations a name.

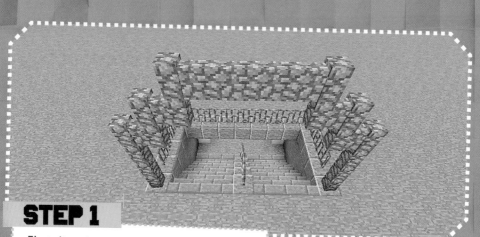

STEP 1

First dig a hole nine blocks wide, seven blocks long, and five blocks deep. Line three sides of the top of the hole with polished andesite. Decorate the last side with an archway made from cobblestone wall and build steps down from it using five stone brick stair blocks placed corner to corner. Add a line of polished andesite blocks down the center with iron bars on top for railings. Then line the sides of the stairs with stone blocks.

STEP 2

Now, two blocks down from the bottom of your steps, hollow out a hole nineteen blocks wide (six blocks out from either side of your steps), 30 blocks long, and six blocks high (stop one block below the surface). Line your hole with stone and add a seven block wide platform all the way down the middle.

railtrack

railtrack

platform

ROCK AND ROLL

There are different ways of building an underground rail network but the completed rail systems run on the same thing: electricity.

« DIGGING TUNNELS »

There are two main ways to build tunnels in the real world.

One way is to open up the ground and build the tunnel in a trench, then cover it over again afterward. This is the cheapest and easiest way. But that's not possible in a city that has already been built, where all the ground is occupied.

The other way is to use a massive boring machine (because it bores a hole, not because it's dull). This machine grinds away the spoil (dirt and rock) in front of it and moves slowly forward into the space it has excavated. The spoil is carried from the front of the machine to the back to be taken away.

All tunnels need strong supports in the walls and roof to prevent them collapsing inward. The weight of soil, rock, and buildings above a tunnel puts a lot of pressure on the roof, so it needs to be really strong.

ELECTRIC RAILS

《 》

Real subway trains run on electric rails. Electricity can only flow through a completed circuit.

A circuit needs a source of power (such as a battery) and components (such as copper wire) to conduct electricity.

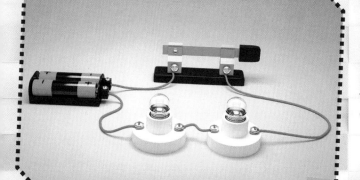

Spoil coming out of the back end of a boring machine as it drills a hole underground.

An underground rail network is a much larger electrical circuit. Instead of wire, metal tracks carry electricity. To complete the circuit, the train makes contact with a "third rail" which lies between or alongside the two main rails. The train acts like a switch, completing or breaking the circuit to make power flow or stop. When the circuit is complete, the electricity drives the train's motors and that turns the wheels—and the train moves.

STEP 3

Line the side of the tunnel with quartz blocks. Add a row of stone brick stairs at the bottom. Two blocks up, add another row, this time upside down. At the top, add a row of stone brick slabs, two blocks wide.

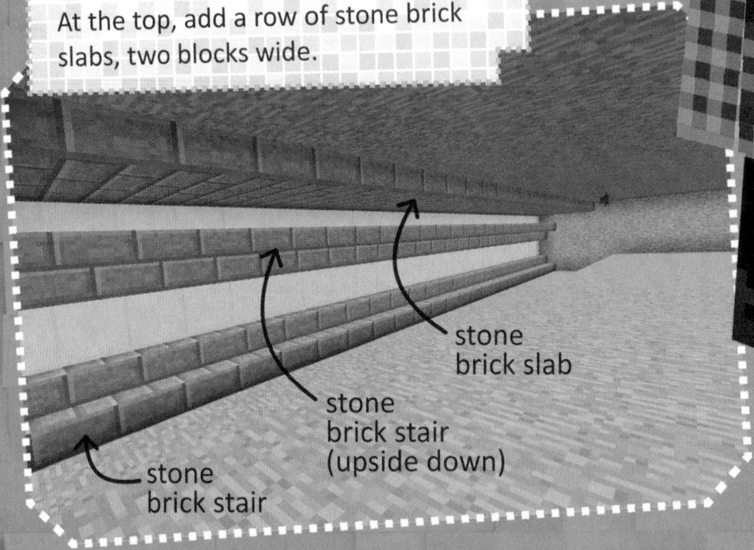

stone
brick slab

stone
brick stair
(upside down)

stone
brick stair

STEP 4

The trains will run on powered rails. Replace the stone floor next to the stone brick stairs with redstone blocks and lay powered rail on top. The redstone will provide power to the rails to move the minecarts.

STEP 5

Lay a row of stone brick stairs along the other side of the track. Then replace the row of stone at the edge of the platform with yellow concrete. This line marks the edge of the platform so that passengers can see it clearly and won't fall onto the rails.

STEP 6

At the end of the platform, continue the tunnel walls by extending the three rows of stone brick stairs and adding another row two blocks above platform level to create a rounded tunnel for your track to run along. Remove the blocks inside your tunnel walls to create your tunnel. Make it as long as you want to.

REFLECT AND CONNECT

Light is scarce underground but there are clever ways to increase light levels, and planning your underground system carefully could help with that.

≪ LIGHT, DARK, AND COLORS ≫

Have you noticed that a room painted white seems much lighter than a room painted a dark color, even if they are both the same size and have the same windows or lighting? That's because pale colors, and particularly white, reflect a lot of light. The light bounces off the pale walls and makes the room lighter. If the walls are dark, they absorb light.

When you look at a colored object, the color you see is the light reflected from the surface. So a red rug absorbs light of lots of colors, but reflects red light. White light is a mix of all colors, as you can tell if you split it into a spectrum. (A rainbow works in the same way: the water drops split the light into its different colors.) By giving your station a white roof, you will help to keep it light and it will reflect the light coming from the glowstone lamps.

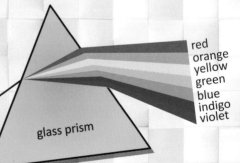

white light

glass prism

red
orange
yellow
green
blue
indigo
violet

EXTEND YOUR RAILS

You can make more stations in exactly the same way at other locations in your city. If you want to join up the stations, you will need to plan the route carefully before you begin. Use squared paper to draw a scale plan of the city, then draw in the route you want your train line to take and where you will put the stations.

It's easiest to make a single straight line that joins all your stations, running from one end of the city to the other. You will need to count carefully as you dig the tunnels to make sure everything joins up properly.

Make sure you build the entrances facing the right way, so that the platform is between the two tracks and not across them!

An underground rail system has different lines that connect all the different parts of the city.

STEP 7

Repeat Steps 3–6 on the other side of the platform (and at the other ends of the platforms) so that rails and tunnels on both sides continue in both directions. Note: from this angle you can't see the redstone tracks but don't worry, they are there!

STEP 8

You need to make sure that the roof is not going to fall in on the unfortunate passengers! Every six blocks on both sides of the platform, use iron blocks to build columns to support the roof.

STEP 9

As it is, this won't be a very nice station to wait in. It will be dark underground and there's nowhere to sit. Let's make it nicer. Change the ceiling to quartz, which is lighter and will reflect more light down to the platform. Then midway between each pair of roof supports, hang a glowstone block from the ceiling to provide lighting. Use quartz slabs to build benches three blocks long between the supports, remembering to leave a gap at each end so that people can walk through to get on the trains.

SHOPPING MALL

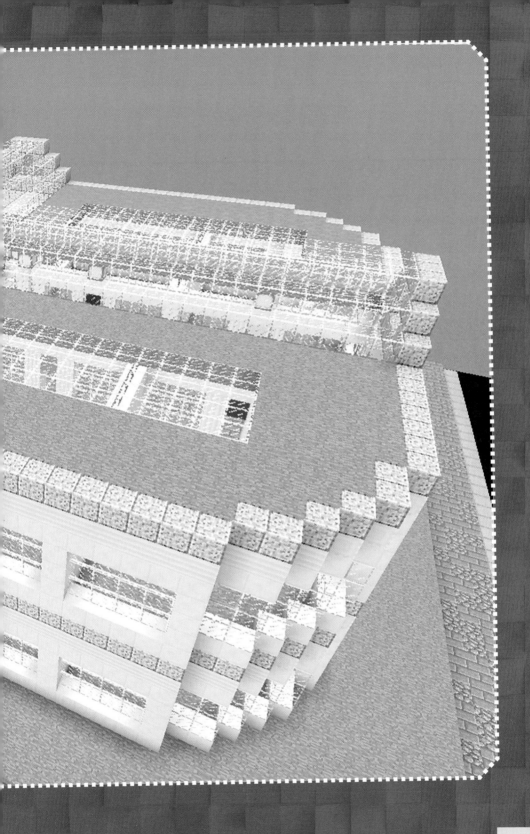

SHOPPING MALL INSPIRATION

TOP TIP!

Make sure there are lots of ways for shoppers to get from one floor to another. Elevators, escalators, and stairs should be in several places throughout the build.

Shopping malls have ultra-modern architecture—you'll need plenty of white blocks.

Shopping malls are divided into "units," which will be filled with shops selling all kinds of different things. You will need to make sure each unit has a nice, big window to fill with goods to tempt customers in to buy their stock. It's important to think about light sources—a glass roof is a good idea. And you also need to consider the route people will take through the mall. Will they be arriving on foot, by car, or public transport? Make sure there are enough external doors for crowds of people to get through when the mall opens.

Think about plants to improve the air quality.

Courtesy of Hilltest and Omgtrees

SHOPPING MALL

People in your city will want somewhere to buy the things that they need, so let's give them a shopping mall. This one will go next to your red brick apartment building, across the road from your stadium. It's light and airy—the perfect place to shop.

≪ SHOP FLOORS ≫

This is the plan for the shopping mall. There are two floors with the same layout, except that the second floor doesn't have doors to the outside world.

STEP 1

With the plan as your guide, start laying the outside walls of the shopping mall using quartz block. Leave a gap at the front for the entrance. Then mark out the internal walls and add paths using double stone slabs.

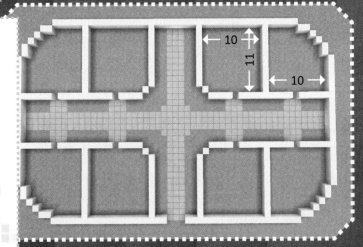

10

11

10

STEP 2

Add a fountain in the middle of the shopping mall. Use quartz stairs for the base, with pillar quartz in the middle. Add glass panes around the top edge of the quartz stairs; this will make the water flow the way you want it to later on. Add stone slabs around the bottom of the fountain to contain the falling water and stop it from going everywhere! Add water by tapping the top of the fountain with a water bucket.

MATERIALS

STEP 3

Now build a framework for all of the walls using more quartz. Make it five blocks high, leaving big spaces for the windows. Shops have large display windows to attract customers. Remember to leave doorways in the internal walls so that people can get into the shops. The doorways to each shop line up with the paths. Add a row of pillar quartz above the main entrance.

STEP 4

Now add pillar quartz to either side of each shop doorway. Then add the windows. Fill in all the large windows with glass panes. Where there are gaps at the corners of walls, use glass blocks because you can't place glass panes across a diagonal.

SHAPE AND MATTER

Rounded shapes and water features are both possible in the blocky world of Minecraft—they just take planning and preparation.

≪ MAKING CURVES ≫

The shops have curved corners, but these are not easy to make with only straight-sided bricks. You can think of a curved line as being made up of lots of very tiny, short, straight lines. When the lines are short enough, the line looks curved, but if you zoom in or make the lines longer, it gets blocky. In Minecraft, all curves are blocky. If you want to plan a build with curved lines, the best way to work out the curves is to use graph paper.

Coloring in the blocks that your curved shape goes through provides a plan for your Minecraft build.

SOLID, LIQUID, GAS

There are three states in which matter exists in the world around us. It can be a solid, a liquid, or a gas. All the blocks you have used so far are solids. Solids hold their own shape. Liquids don't hold their own shape, so have to be held in a container. The fountain has a low wall around it because otherwise the water would flow all over the floor, just like it would in real life. Liquids flow downhill. A gas does not hold its own shape, but will fill any space it is in. While liquids flow downward, gases usually spread out in all directions.

water block

grass block

STEP 5

Customers will need to be able to go up to the next floor. Opposite the main entrance, four blocks back from the base of the fountain, build your staircase from quartz stairs edged with stone brick. Make it five blocks wide and seven blocks high.

STEP 6

Add two rows of pillar quartz to the top of the outside wall, one inside the other, and finish the ceiling with a single layer of stone. Add a layer of glass panes along the top of the interior walls with sea lanterns above each doorway and corner. Finally, put a different color of concrete block at the top of each shop doorway.

Copy the layout for the internal walls from Step 1. This time use stone bricks for the paths. Make sure there's a 6x3 hole around the staircase. Put a safety barrier made from glass panes around the staircase hole, leaving two blocks clear at the back to give people access to the stairs. Follow Step 2 again to make your second fountain.

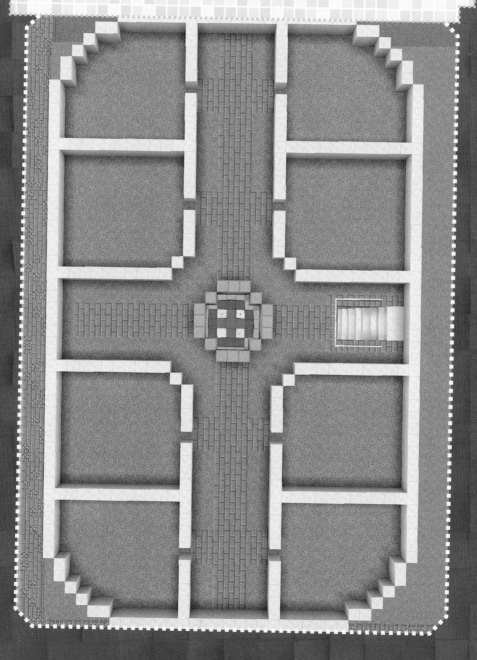

STEP 8

Follow Steps 3, 4, and 6 again to recreate the entire ground floor layout on the new floor.

STEP 9

Then, outside, add a row of polished diorite seven blocks up, and a row of pillar quartz followed by a row of polished diorite around the top of the outside walls, and complete the roof using stone.

Lastly, add light! Five blocks in from the edges of the roof, replace four 5x15 sections of stone with glass panes. Use polished diorite to create the arches for the atrium windows. Then use glass blocks to glaze the atrium windows and make arched windows all along the length and width of the roof.

PARKING GARAGE

The parking garage is nex
the shopping mall so th
customers from out of tow
easily go shopping. This on
two stories, but you can ac
many extra floors as you

SLOPES A
STAIRS

In a real parking garage, t
between the two levels w
a gentle slope so that cars
easily from one floor to th
In Minecraft, stairs always
45-degree angle and it's i
to lay a flat surface over t
A slope this steep would b
dangerous in a parking ga
Next time you visit one, lo
to see how gentle the slop

STEP 1

Four blocks back from the road, lay a 63x39 perimeter using stone slabs with a 3x3 square of stone bricks in each corner. Replace the grass blocks inside the perimeter with black concrete and mark out parking spaces using white concrete. Each parking space is three blocks wide and five blocks long. Create a dotted line for where the ramp will go up to the next floor.

STEP 2

Next to the dotted line, build the ramp from seven rows of black and white concrete blocks placed corner to corner (diagonally). Make these rows nine blocks long, the same length as the dotted line. Add stone bricks at the side to create a safety barrier—we don't want any cars to drive off the edge.

On the same level as the top of your ramp, lay a floor of black and white concrete, with the same markings as shown. Leave a 10x7 gap around the ramp. Edge this gap with stone bricks on three sides to form another safety barrier. On top of this floor, build a perimeter wall made from stone slabs with 3x3 stone brick squares in the corners.

STEP 4

Build up the stone brick in the corners to join the ground floor with the top of the parking garage. Underneath the perimeter wall made from stone slabs at the top of the parking garage, add a row of stone brick blocks all the way around.

STEP 5

Add a safety barrier around the top floor by adding another layer of stone bricks on top of your 3x3 corner squares and joining them up with a single row of stone brick all around the perimeter.

PARK

PARK INSPIRATION

Courtesy of 0KoenigseggAgera0

Central Park, New York

You can have a lot of fun planning your park. Minecraft is full of different trees and plants, plus you can build small sculptures and monuments, and add a lake or water feature.

Why not take a walk in your local park to get some inspiration? Is it formal or more relaxed? How much space is there for sports games? Count up the number of benches for people to sit and relax on. Look at where flowers have been planted and which colors look best together. And don't forget about small children—make sure you have an area with swings, slides, and plenty of room to run around. You could even include a skate park. It might be nice to add a small cafe too, so visitors can grab a quick drink and snack.

Courtesy of 0KoenigseggAgera0

PARK

Whether they want to walk their dog, play with friends, go for a run, or just sit in the sun, the people of your city will love going to the park. It's right next to the shopping mall so that people can get some fresh air and chill after shopping.

≪ FREE PLAY ≫

Unlike the other builds, you don't need to stick strictly to the instructions to make sure all the parts go together. You can put different elements of the park in different places and it will still work out. Maybe you want a bigger playground, or to change the ice rink to a boating lake? The choice is yours!

MATERIALS

STEP 1

The L-shaped playground sits in the far corner of the park opposite the shopping mall. Prepare the ground by replacing 27x15 grass blocks with sand, leaving one 6x9 corner untouched. Surround your L-shape using oak fence with oak fence gate along one short side.

FOR REAL!

Sand provides a soft landing surface that doesn't get muddy, and fencing keeps animals out and stops small children from running off.

STEP 2

Build your slide from spruce stairs and oak wood planks. Make it three blocks high and two blocks wide with fence on either side and ladders at the back.

For the swings, build a frame from oak fence and each swing from iron bars and oak wood slabs.

sticky piston

TOP TIP!

These Minecraft versions of playground favorites are just for display, but you can experiment with pistons, sticky pistons, and redstone to create an all-new playground ride.

STEP 4

Make the frame for the zip wire using oak fence. Use iron bars and oak wood slabs to make the seat.

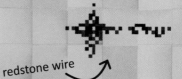

piston

redstone wire

GO WITH THE FLOW

Friction and temperature can have a dramatic effect on how objects behave; from how fast or slowly something moves to whether it exists as a liquid, solid, or gas.

« FRICTION »

When you walk on a rough surface, such as grass, it locks together with the surface of your shoes, creating friction (a force that resists movement). An ice rink and ice skates both have smooth surfaces. When one smooth surface meets another, there is very little friction so you slip and slide quickly and easily.

But even though the surface of an ice rink is smooth, there is enough friction to melt it slightly. This makes it even more slippery because the thin layer of water evens out the small ridges and dips from people's skates. Which you want on an ice rink, but not when you're walking!

« N-ICE SUMMER? »

Ice rinks pop up everywhere in the winter. Like a freezer, they use electricity to keep the ice frozen. In the summer, with all that sunshine and warmth, an ice rink would use up a huge amount of electricity. Luckily, the Minecraft sun won't melt your ice rink so you can have it all year.

Skis travel fast on snow because both surfaces are very smooth.

« ICE, WATER, STEAM »

Ice is water that has frozen (or become solid) because it's gone below its freezing point of 32 °F (0 °C). As ice warms up, it melts. This means there's always a thin layer of water on the surface of an ice rink because there's always warmer air above it.

If water is heated to its boiling point of 212 °F (100 °C), it starts to bubble and escape as steam. Think of a boiling kettle or pan. When steam hits a cold surface, such as a window, it condenses, forming drops of liquid again.

This picture shows H_2O as ice (a solid), water (a liquid), and steam (a gas).

STEP 5

Use oak wood for the center of the seesaw and oak wood planks for the sides.

STEP 6

Next, create the ice rink. It's in the corner nearest the parking garage. Starting six blocks from each edge of the park, dig out a 20x30 rectangle and round off the corners. Then fill the hole with ice.

STEP 7

Edge the ice with a safety barrier made from hay bales, leaving spaces for the entrance and exit. Put oak fence across the entrance and exit, and make lighting from oak fence and glowstone.

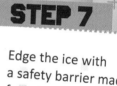

STEP 8

In the corner opposite the parking garage and next to the ice rink, make a decorative water feature. Use stone block to create an irregular pile of rocks, with different levels for the water to cascade down from. Dig a hole for your pool in front of the rocks. Touch the top with a water bucket to start the water flowing.

Right click with your shovel to create a path. Replace grass with dirt blocks, and sprinkle seeds and bone meal to grow flowers and crops.

PERFECT PATTERNS

Designers and architects think very carefully about the shapes they use to decorate and cover surfaces. From paving slabs to roof tiles, there are tessellating shapes everywhere.

≪ TILES AND TESSELLATIONS ≫

The plaza is tiled with shapes that fit together perfectly. Any shape that can be repeated to fill an area without leaving any gaps is said to "tessellate." All wall and floor tiles are made of tessellating shapes, such as squares, rectangles, and hexagons.

Equilateral triangles, hexagons and squares tessellate.

These are not the only shapes that tessellate, though. There are some you might not immediately think of:

Some irregular shapes tessellate.

A pattern can even be made from two or more shapes that tessellate together:

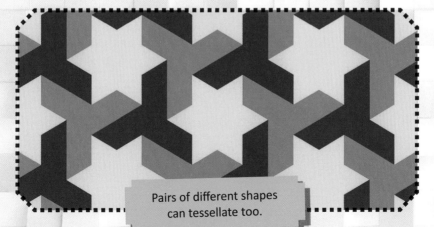

Pairs of different shapes can tessellate too.

In the corner of the park closest to the shopping mall, you're going to build a plaza with decorative paving and a fountain. Around 15 blocks in from the edges of the park, build the base for the fountain. Dig out a circle with a radius of six blocks (that's the distance from the edge to the center) and line it with stone bricks. Add a stone brick wall around the outside edge to keep the water in.

STEP 11

Now add paving around the fountain in a symmetrical design, using different colors. We have placed polished andesite and polished granite in horizontal, diagonal, and vertical rows that are eight blocks long, but you could use different blocks and create your own design.

STEP 12

To follow this design, lay polished diorite around the edges of your rows, making it two blocks wide around the straight edges and one block wide around the diagonals.

STEP 13

Fill in the gaps with P-shaped designs made from stone brick and polished granite, and finish off the edges with more polished diorite.

THE STUFF OF LIFE

Everything needs help to grow, develop, and thrive—in both Minecraft and the real world. Plants provide food for lots of animals (and people) so let's find out more about them...

« HOW PLANTS WORK »

Most plants have roots, a stem, and leaves. Many also have flowers some of the time.

The roots keep the plant firmly in place in the ground. Water and nutrients from the soil enter the plant through the roots. They travel along the stem to reach the growing tips of the plant and the leaves.

The leaves contain a substance called chlorophyll, which uses the energy from sunlight, water carried up from the roots, and gases from air to make food for the plant. Chlorophyll is green, which is why most plants are green.

To reproduce, many plants make seeds. Others split apart or grow new plants from roots that spread underground. Plants that make seeds have flowers.

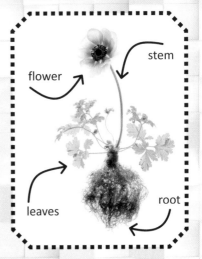

flower
stem
leaves
root

WHAT PLANTS NEED

In Minecraft, we can make plants and flowers grow by sprinkling bone meal on the grass. In the real world, plants and flowers grow from seed, so to add flowers to your grass you would need to sow some seed. Plants also need sunlight, water, and soil in order to grow.

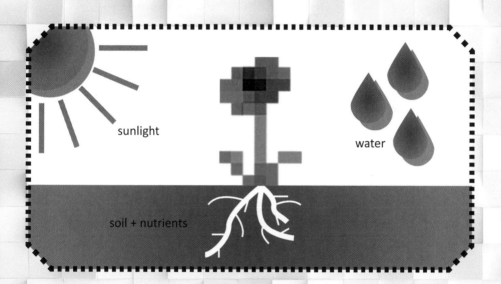

sunlight

water

soil + nutrients

BRILLIANT BONE

Farmers and gardeners often use fertilizer to help plants grow better. Fertilizer is a special plant food that has nutrients (useful chemicals) in it. Bone meal, which is made from ground-up animal bones, is a great fertilizer. The nutrients in it are more concentrated (stronger) than the nutrients in the soil so they help plants to grow strong and healthy.

bone meal

STEP 14

Add a pyramid of stone blocks three blocks high and five blocks wide to the middle of the fountain. Then right click the top with a water bucket and water will start to flow down into the base.

STEP 15

Add paths to help people find their way around the park. To turn grass into a grass path, right-click on the grass block with a shovel. The paths should be winding rather than straight, and they should link all parts of the park.

STEP 16

Finally, plant trees around the park, wherever you think they will look good. To grow longer grass and flowers, sprinkle bone meal around the park.

ROADS

You can connect your city to towns, villages, or out-of-city attractions such as a theme park with bigger roads, just like in real life. Here's a simple way to build a two-lane road toward your next incredible build...

STEP 1

The first thing you need to do is figure out what sizes to make everything. Here we are making four lanes of five blocks wide, with extra space in the middle for a crash barrier. Use white blocks to mark your lanes.

STEP 2

Repeat Step 1 until your road is long enough. Make a dashed line down the middle of each pair of lanes and use solid lines for the borders.

Now add a crash barrier to the middle. These are built to stop vehicles from bumping into each other.

STEP 4

Adding a stone wall or fence along each side of your highway creates a nice decorative touch. Simply add an extra strip of blocks down both sides of your highway.

STEP 5

One of the best things about road trips is getting to see the sights. Add some trees to make our road more scenic. In this example we've built tree bases from birch wood.

STEP 6

Once you're happy with your choice of wood, add leaves. It's a good idea to match your leaf type with your wood type. Aim to build something like a sphere around the top of the log.

STEP 7

Time to get creative! Make some pals for your first tree in this step. Place them randomly and try giving them different heights. Make as many or as few trees as you like; it's your highway!

STEP 8

Now add some plants and flowers. There are plenty to choose from, so go wild! Here we have spaced the flowers randomly around our trees and added grass and bushes.

STEP 9

You can make a pedestrian bridge for those people who prefer two legs to four wheels! Make a base on one side of the highway, wide enough for a few people to walk across.

STEP 10

Using the base, start to build up stairs. Increase the block height by one each time, moving from the outside and building toward the highway. Add stair blocks of your choice along each level.

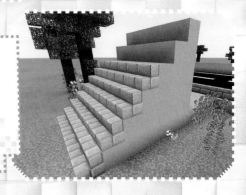

Build another strip of blocks one block taller on each side of the stairs. Remember, the colors we have used are just an example, so feel free to choose your own.

STEP 12

Once you are happy with your stairs, finish them off by adding another wall or fence along each side. Repeat the stairs on the other side of the highway and join them with a bridge across the middle.

BONUS TIP

When building your road, or highway, there are a couple of things to keep in mind. Lanes should be kept an equal width, but the road can be any length or shape. Be as creative as you like and try to think about what features you want to add to it. Have fun!

WELCOME TO THE THEME PARK!

In this section we'll show you how to build a fantastic Minecraft theme park with all the attractions of a real-life park, such as a Ferris wheel, a bouncy castle, and a roller coaster. If you're ready to have fun, let's start building!

AND HERE'S HOW IT LOOKS FROM ABOVE!

We've put the builds in an order that has the easier ones first, but you don't have to do them in that order. As long as you stick to the plan on pages 204–5, and you start by making the paths and fences first that divide up the areas, you can build the rides in any order and the theme park will fit together perfectly.

DOING MORE

We don't want to limit your imagination! Use the book as your starting point and make an enormous theme park, if you like. If you want to add more things, either wait until you've finished or add them outside the area covered by the plan. For instance, if you want to create an arena for bumper cars, you might put it behind the roller coaster. All you'll have to do then is adjust the fence around the park to include your new

attraction. But if you put new items in the area covered by the plan, you'll find the builds won't all fit.

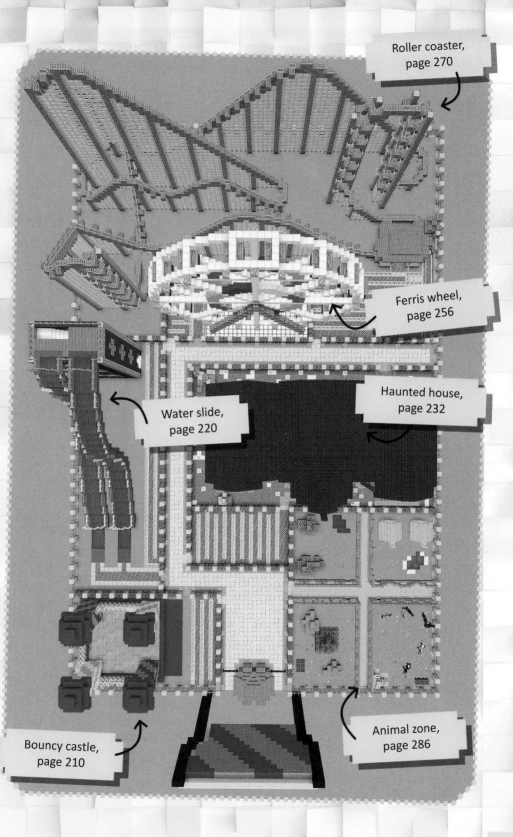

Roller coaster, page 270

Ferris wheel, page 256

Haunted house, page 232

Water slide, page 220

Bouncy castle, page 210

Animal zone, page 286

THEME PARK INSPIRATION

A big wheel is a popular central focus for a theme park.

TOP TIP!

Think carefully about the positioning of each ride in your theme park—make sure a smaller ride isn't hidden behind a big one so that everything can be seen.

You can build a roller coaster, but it can't be quite as twisty and turny as this one!

Even if you've never been to a theme park, you probably know the kinds of things you'll find there —plenty of cool rides, concession stands, picnic areas, maybe even a petting zoo. But don't forget the restrooms—everyone needs to take a break from time to time.

The first thing to do when looking for inspiration is think BIG! Reach for the sky with your rides and make sure you're satisfying everyone's need for speed! There are thousands of roller coasters around the world, from old-school wooden ones to state-of-the-art metal ones perfect for speed demons. You will be restricted by how Minecraft works and the kinds of shapes you can make, but that shouldn't stop you giving your ride an awesome theme.

There are plenty of other people who have built their own Minecraft theme park or fairground—it's a popular project for Minecrafters who need a new challenge. Whereas your city build was full of straight lines, you will have to learn how to form curves and circles in order to master these builds. It might be a bit trickier, but it sure is a lot of fun!

Courtesy of www.apk-dl.com

Make sure your theme park is colorful and fun!

TOP TIP!

If there's one thing nobody likes about theme parks, it's the waiting in line! Make sure you allow plenty of room, and maybe add in some distractions.

ON THE GROUND?

This plan shows the areas set aside for the different rides at your park. As long as you follow it carefully, your theme park will really come together.

《 FOOTPRINT 》

grass block

The area on the ground that is taken up by the theme park is called its footprint. Sometimes, the footprint is larger than the bottom layer of the build. For example, some rides are narrow at the bottom, but expand out once they start moving.

SCALE

Architects, quantity surveyors, and builders work to detailed plans. They use a consistent scale so they are able to work out the measurements for all the parts that they're building.

For example, a plan might have a scale of 1:100, which would mean that each 1 inch measured on the plan corresponds with 100 inches in the actual building.

AREA

The area of a shape is the space it covers. Unlike the city, this theme park is a rectangle, so its area is the length of the long side multiplied by the length of the short side:

124 x 83 = 10,292 blocks.

Area has two dimensions, so it's usually measured in "square" units, such as square inches (in^2) or square feet (ft^2).

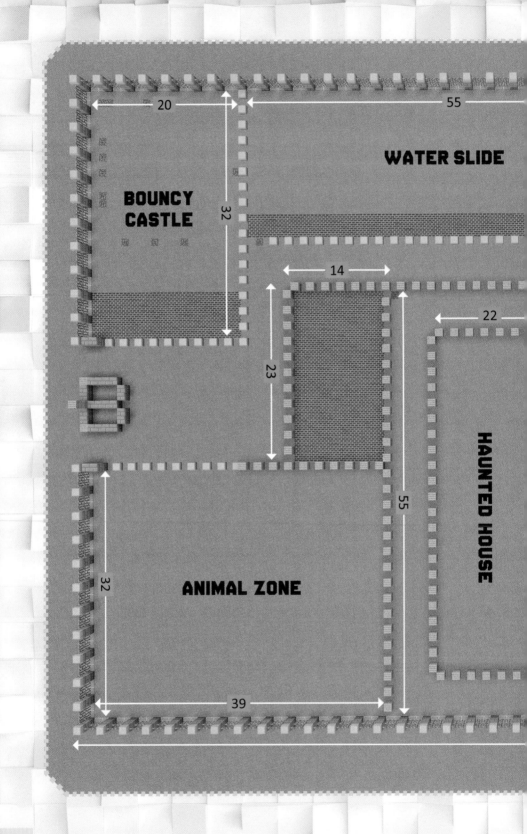

BOUNCY CASTLE

WATER SLIDE

20

55

32

14

23

22

HAUNTED HOUSE

55

ANIMAL ZONE

32

39

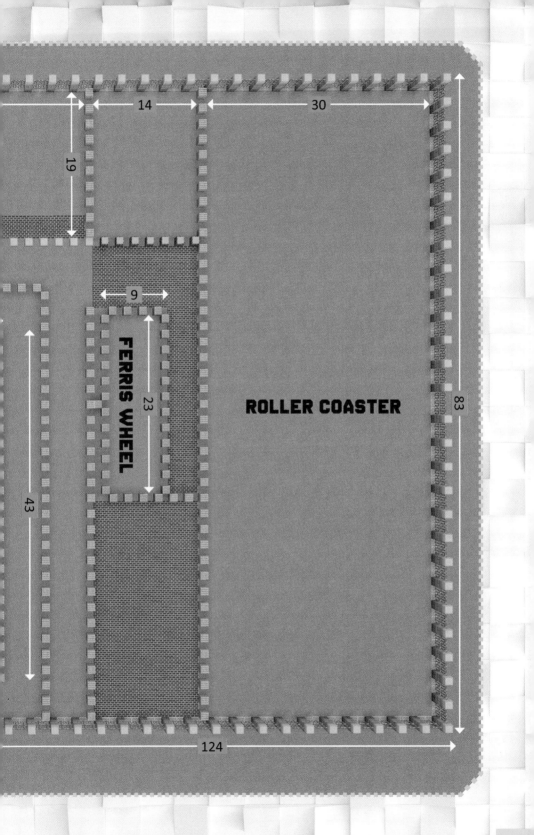

ROLLER COASTER

FERRIS WHEEL

14

30

19

9

23

83

43

124

SETTING THE SCENE

We'll start by marking out all the areas for each build and laying pavement. In real life, surveyors also work out exactly where everything is going to go. Marking the boundaries between rides at this stage makes it easy to see where to start each build.

⟪ GRIDLOCK ⟫

The plan on pages 204–5 shows how much space you will need for each ride. This type of plan is similar to ones that real builders, architects, and designers use. It helps you to see how all the different parts of the theme park fit together. There is a more detailed plan at the start of each build so that you can easily see what sizes to make all the parts.

MATERIALS

STEP 1

Begin by marking out the perimeter of the theme park. Dig up grass blocks and replace them with polished andesite to create a 124x83 rectangle. Knock out a gap in the middle of one short side for the entrance. The gap should be 15 blocks wide, with 34 blocks on either side of it.

STEP 2

Now make a fence around the perimeter. The fence has pillars made of two blocks of stone brick with a stone slab on top. Build pillars in each corner, leave two slabs empty, then add another pillar. Keep going all the way round. Then fill in the gaps with iron bars.

STEP 3

Using the plan on pages 204–5 as a guide, mark out the areas for the different rides, using any blocks you like. This will help you to count up the blocks more easily for each build.

STEP 4

The areas of red paving which you can see in the plan on pages 204–5 are level with the ground, so you will need to dig out a layer one block deep before adding bricks. Double-check the dimensions by counting the blocks: it's important that you get these right so that there's enough space for each build.

STEP 5

Add the 6x7 footprint for the ticket booths using stone bricks and oak wood planks.

BOUNCY CASTLE

BOUNCY CASTLE

What could be more fun than bouncing sky-high on a multicolored castle? This one is just inside the entrance to your theme park, and it's a great first build.

« GETTING STARTED »

Here's the layout for your bouncy castle. Look carefully at the plan and refer back to it as you are building. It has all the dimensions you will need to use. The plan is shown to scale. Your build will have exactly the same proportions as the picture in the plan.

UNREAL!

In Minecraft, slime is bouncy. Your customers might not like the feel of a bouncy castle made entirely of slime, so we've covered it with wool, which is nice and soft—it feels much nicer than slime. The slime will be bouncy, even when it's covered with wool.

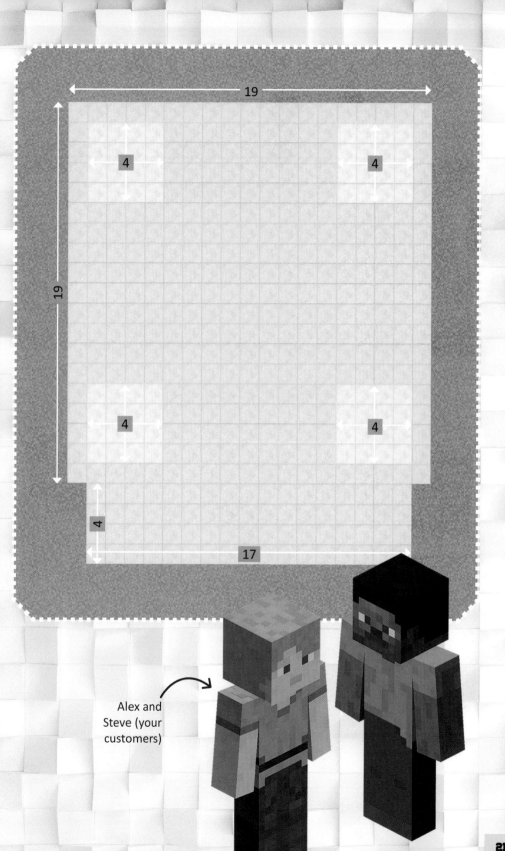

Alex and Steve (your customers)

STEP 1

Mark out a 19x19 square of blocks. Go all around the perimeter laying a single row of red wool. Now fill in the middle with a single layer of slime—it's what will give your bouncy castle its boing!

STEP 2

Dig out a 17x4 rectangle as a landing area to one side. It starts one block in from the edge of the bouncy base. Fill it with a layer of red wool. This is a soft landing area in case anyone bounces right off.

MATERIALS

STEP 3

Build four 4x4 bases for the towers in each corner using colored wool. Create a barrier between the tower bases by adding a row of red wool along three sides. Fill in the middle with wool in any colors and patterns you like. The slime will still be bouncy, but it's nicer to bounce on wool than on slime.

TOP TIP!

People need to be safe in your theme park. You don't want them to bounce off the bouncy castle, so we've put a soft landing area at the front.

IMPORTANT STUFF

Materials can be used to control how we physically feel. They can be used to control light, temperature and even the way we move so that we are more comfortable and secure.

« BOUNCY MATERIALS »

A real bouncy castle is not made of slime and wool. It's made of a rubbery plastic material and it's inflatable. It is filled with air using a giant pump. As you jump on it, the pressure of your body pressing down squeezes some of the air out of the way from underneath you. But it can't go far as the bouncy castle is already full of air. This means you sink a bit, but the air inside pushes back up too, making it bouncy.

Your feet push down, the trapped air pushes back—and you bounce!

WARM AND WOOLY

A material like wool that is warm to the touch is a thermal insulator. This means that heat doesn't travel through it easily. That's why a wooly sweater is good for keeping you warm: the heat of your body can't travel through the wool to the outside air. Materials that are cold to the touch, like metal, are thermal conductors. Metal feels cold because it carries heat away from your body.

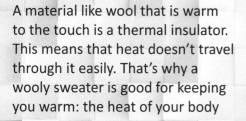

A metal baking tray conducts heat so you have to wear oven mitts.

The plastic handle on a frying pan doesn't conduct heat—no need to protect your hands.

STEP 4

Build each of your towers ten blocks high. Use any colors and patterns you like. Leave one block missing from the top corner of each tower—this shape will help you form the base of the turrets you are going to build next.

STEP 5

For your turrets, place a 2x2 square of red wool in each corner of the tower. These will fill the missing blocks and stick out around to the top of the tower. Join these together by placing rows of four blocks above them. Finish off with a 4x4 square and a 2x2 square on top.

STEP 6

Finally, on top of the red wool edges of the castle, add a barrier of cobweb three blocks high. Build up the ends by adding an L-shape made from three cobweb blocks. Cobweb is just the right material to use for a protective barrier, since people can see through it but not bounce through it.

Staggering blocks creates shadows and breaks up the... well, blockiness of Minecraft!

« LOCATION, LOCATION »

The water slide is just behind the bouncy castle. Look carefully at the theme park plan on pages 204–5 and refer back to it as you are building. Make sure you build it in the right place and facing the right way: the water slides come down toward the bouncy castle so visitors can see their friends bouncing as they hurtle downward.

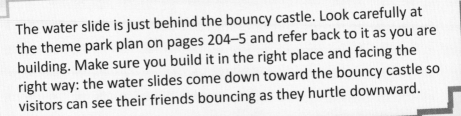

WATER SLIDE

After all that bouncing, your visitors might want to cool off with a good splash. A water slide is great on a warm day—you're bound to get at least a little bit wet!

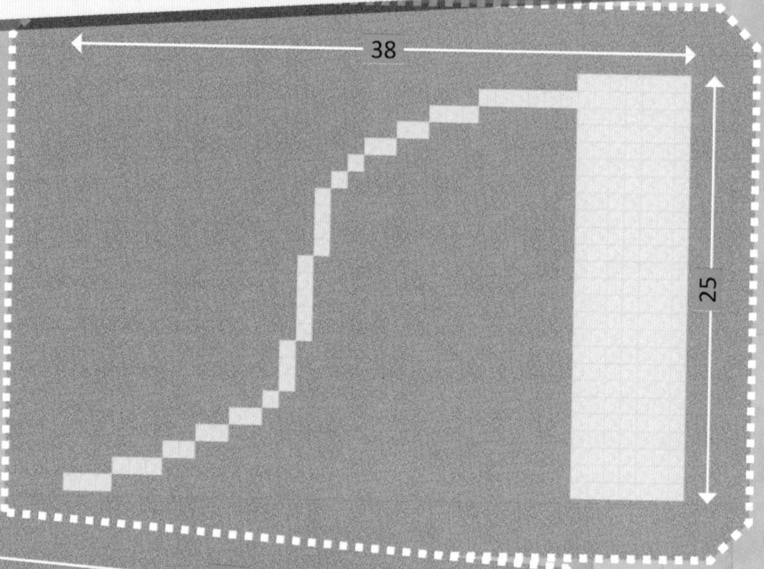

38

25

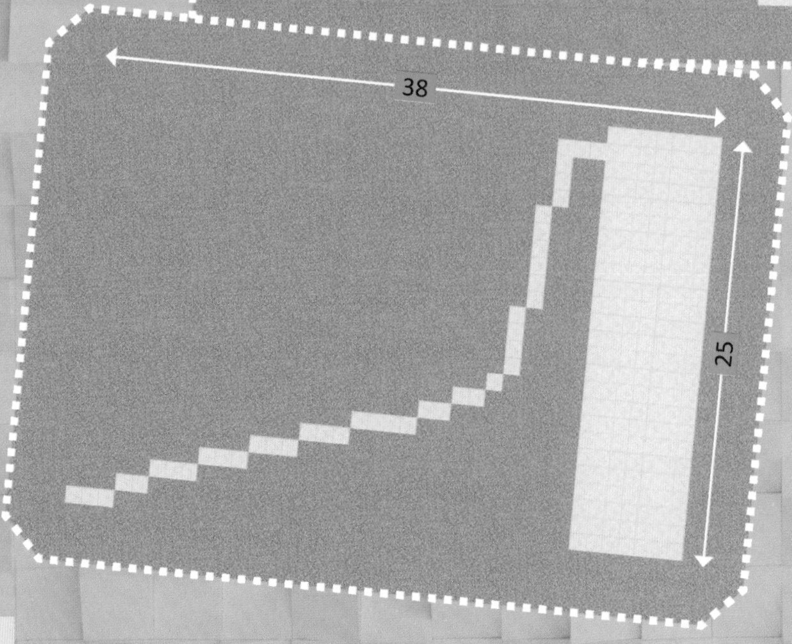

38

25

SHAPE AND SPEED

The shape of a surface and what it is made of affect the speed at which objects—and even air and water—can move over it.

⟪ CURVING IN AND OUT ⟫

The convex curve on this mirror gives drivers a wider view.

The curves of the slides go in different directions, one bending outward and one inward:

We can say that a curve arching outward is convex and one arching inward is concave. But whether a curve is convex or concave depends on which side of it you are standing.

One way round this is to call the curves "concave upward" and "concave downward" (or convex downward and convex upward!). The magenta slide is concave downward; the blue slide is concave upward.

FAST AND SLOW

Going down these two slides would be very different! People on the water slide will go fastest where the slope is steepest, so on the magenta ride they will start slowly and then really speed up, whereas on the blue slide they will go super-fast straight away. Which would you rather do?

The concave curve on this spoon helps it hold liquid.

MATERIALS

≪ READY STEADY ≫

We're going to begin by building the framework so that you can see the general shape of the water slide, and then we'll fill it in. Look at the theme park footprint to make sure you start in the right place.

≪ UNDER AND OVER ≫

Although the tower and the end of the slide are on the ground, much of the slide is elevated so there is empty space underneath it. On the plan, this space is still shown as part of its layout (the area it occupies) so no one puts a tall sign or lamppost there. The tower has steps inside so that visitors can go up, and windows to let some light in—you don't want them to trip on the stairs.

STEP 1

Count out a 7x13 rectangle one block in from the perimeter fence and the back of the water slide section of the plan. This will be the base for your wooden tower. Place a 25x1 oak wood column in each corner. Join up the tops of the columns on each short side of the rectangle. Use the plans on page 222–3 to help you build the base for each slide from magenta (which looks pink) and light blue hardened clay (which looks purple). At the end of your slides, dig out 5x3x2 blocks of soil and line them with clay for the water to drain into. Add some more clay blocks at the end to finish them off.

STEP 2

It would be good to see some water flowing, so let's take advantage of the magic of the Minecraft world and add it now! Add sides to each slide first so that the water will flow in the right direction and not over the sides of the slides. Then add a water bucket at the top of each slide. Minecraft water will just keep flowing so one bucket will last forever.

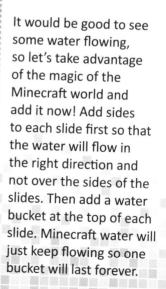

PROPERTIES OF MATERIALS

It's important to choose materials with properties that work well together in your builds.

≪ LIQUIDS AND SOLIDS ≫

Even in Minecraft water flows downward.

Water is a liquid, but all the other parts of your build are solid. Solid materials keep their shape. They might be bendy, soft, or bouncy, but they don't spread out as soon as you put them down. Liquids take the shape of their container. If you tip over a cup of water, it won't stay cup-shaped—it will make a wide, shallow puddle. Liquids can't be piled up or cut into pieces.

GRAVITY

Water always flows from a higher place to a lower place, always going downhill (or over an edge, like a waterfall).

Water follows the shape of the rocks underneath it as it flows downward.

Water at the bottom of the slide stops flowing and fills the space available.

STEP 3

Visitors need to get to the top of the slides, so it's time to build the walls of the tower and put stairs inside. If you use different types of wood, you can build a pattern into the tower. We have used acacia and spruce planks here. Include windows to let light in so that no one trips on the stairs. Add window bars from oak fence.

STEP 4

Once the walls are in place, build stairs around the inside walls of the tower. Use quartz stairs for the steps and quartz block for the landings where the stairs turn. Don't forget to leave a doorway so that people can get in.

STEP 5

It's nearly done now—time for some finishing touches. First, add some fencing and two archways around the top of the slide. Then add more fencing along the edges of each slide (you don't want any visitors falling off!) and two more archways at the bottom. Use different types of wood to add interest. We have used jungle fence for the top of the slide and oak, birch, and spruce for the sides and the bottom.

STEP 6

Last of all, finish the paving at the end of the slide and down the side with bricks and stone slabs. Add oak fence to keep the waiting line in order. Then build a perimeter fence in the same style as the theme park perimeter fence using stone brick, stone slabs, iron bars, and birch leaves.

HAUNTED HOUSE

What better place to chill out after all that bouncing and sliding than a spooky, haunted house? On second thoughts, it might not be so relaxing...

MATERIALS

<< **SPOOKY CENTRAL** >>

The haunted house is right in the middle of the theme park. It casts a dark shadow over the fun and games, daring your visitors to step inside. There's more going on inside than you can see from the outside. You'll need to dig a dungeon (what creepy house doesn't have a dungeon?) and separate the rooms above ground. Who knows what visitors will bump into once they are inside?

witch

cave spider

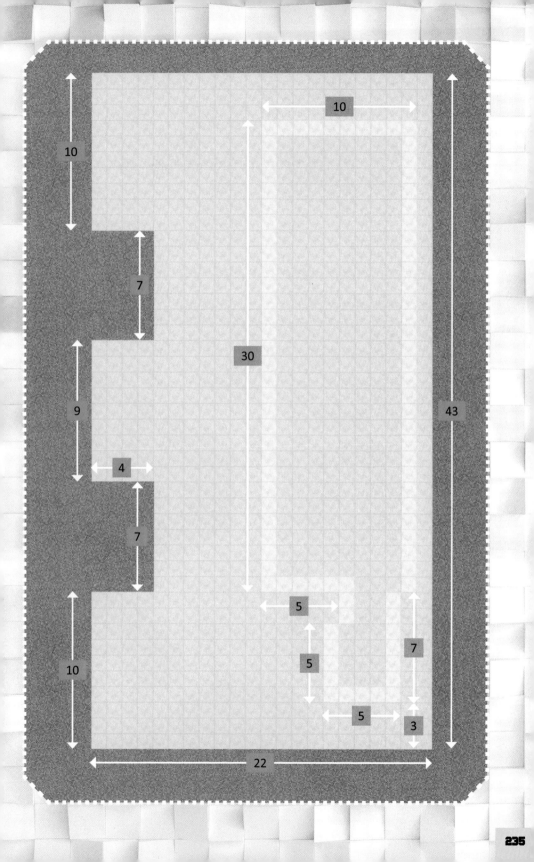

WHAT ON EARTH?

Building usually starts in the dirt, but have you ever really thought about what mud is made of, or what builders do with the mud they dig up from the ground?

≪ DIG THE DIRT ≫

The blocks you remove when you dig down are soil, covered with grass. In the real world, soil is a mix of tiny stones, rotting and broken down plant matter, animal waste, and tiny microscopic organisms (living things), all held together with some water. It's more complicated—and important—than it looks.

grass block

shovel

THE VOLUME OF A HOLE

In Minecraft, soil just disappears if you dig it out. But if someone was really building an underground dungeon, they would have to dig out the soil and move it somewhere or pile it up. The volume of soil removed will be the same as the volume of the hole. You can work out the volume of soil removed to make your dungeon by dividing it into 3D rectangular shapes (cuboids) and working out the volume of each. You could divide this dungeon into three parts: the main room, the short narrow passageway, and the wider area by the ladder. The volume is:

length x width x height

Add the volume of all three areas together to get the total volume of the dungeon (or the soil) you have removed.

STEP 1

Using the plan on page 235 as a guide, dig a dungeon with an exit at one end. Make it four blocks deep—the lowest level will be paved and the dungeon walls will be three blocks high.

torch

Pave the floor with polished andesite. Line the walls with a mix of stone, mossy stone, and cracked stone bricks. Add a ladder at the end of the passageway.

Give each dungeon cell a 5x4 floor area and add cobwebs, a bed, and slime. Use iron bars, stone bricks, and an iron door for the front of each cell and separate them with the same materials you used for the outer walls. Add torches along the walls before you start building on top.

Using the plan on page 235 as a guide, build the footprint for your house. Use cobblestone stairs and oak planks for the perimeter and dark oak planks for the floor. Make sure the dungeon exit comes up in the corner, two blocks in from the back wall, and three blocks in from the side wall.

Mark out where you're going to place your inner walls with oak planks, leaving a space between each block. Build the frame for the outer walls from dark oak wood.

The short columns are nine blocks high and the taller columns are 13 blocks high. Place rows of blocks across the tops of these. The tallest columns for the main entrance are 21 blocks high.

13 blocks high

13 blocks high

9 blocks high

9 blocks high

21 blocks high

dungeon exit

WORKING WITH NATURE

We design buildings to protect us from the elements, but we use materials from nature and need to consider the environment, too.

《 WOODEN HOUSES 》

In many parts of the world, houses are made enitrely or partly of wood.

They are usually built in much the same way as the haunted house, with thick, structural supports at the corners and at intervals along the walls, and then with thinner wood, like planks, filling the gaps. Wood is a thermal insulator—it helps to keep heat in. It's also light and easy to work with since it can be cut with just a saw. Although it's not as strong as brick or stone and it burns easily, wood is a sustainable resource, so that's good for the environment.

Wood is a good building material and it blends well with its environment.

birch wood

WEATHERPROOF

When building a real house, builders try to get the roof on as soon as possible to stop rain falling into the house. They finish the outside walls, and any important inside structural walls, then add the roof. Internal walls and doors, the plumbing, electricity, plastering, and painting are done when the roof is on and the house is secure and dry. In Minecraft, you can carry on building in the rain without any of your materials spoiling or your workers grumbling!

A roof makes a house weatherproof and keeps heat inside.

STEP 3

Fill in the walls using spruce wood planks. Leave space for a door and three windows at the front. Look back at the picture of the house on page 233 to see. One window is above the door, 10 blocks up, and the other two are at the sides, one block up. Fill them with light gray stained glass panes. In the kitchen, lay a patterned floor of black and white tiles using coal block and polished diorite.

Finish the inside of the house before putting the roof on. Start by adding the internal walls using dark oak planks, with an iron block wall in the kitchen. Then add torches at regular intervals throughout. Use polished andesite and bookshelf to create your library. Add a desk in the corner made from bookshelf and oak wood slabs with a lever to open the iron door next to it. (When you add your doors later, make sure they are all made from iron to keep the mobs contained.)

WORKING UNDER PRESSURE

Pistons are versatile in Minecraft but they are usually part of an engine, not a table!

« PISTONS AT WORK »

Pistons live inside a cylinder in an engine within, for example, a car. They move backward and forward very quickly when pressure is put on them.

This pressure comes from expanding gas, which usually comes from burning fuel, such as gasoline.

When pistons move backward and forward, they turn a crankshaft which is connected to the car's wheels. The movement of the crankshaft is then transferred to the wheels and the car moves.

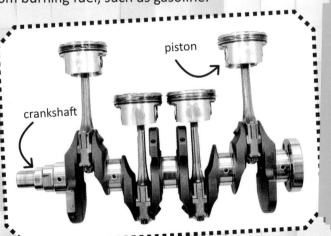

piston

crankshaft

These four pistons inside a car's cylinder move up and down, which turns the crankshaft and makes the wheels move.

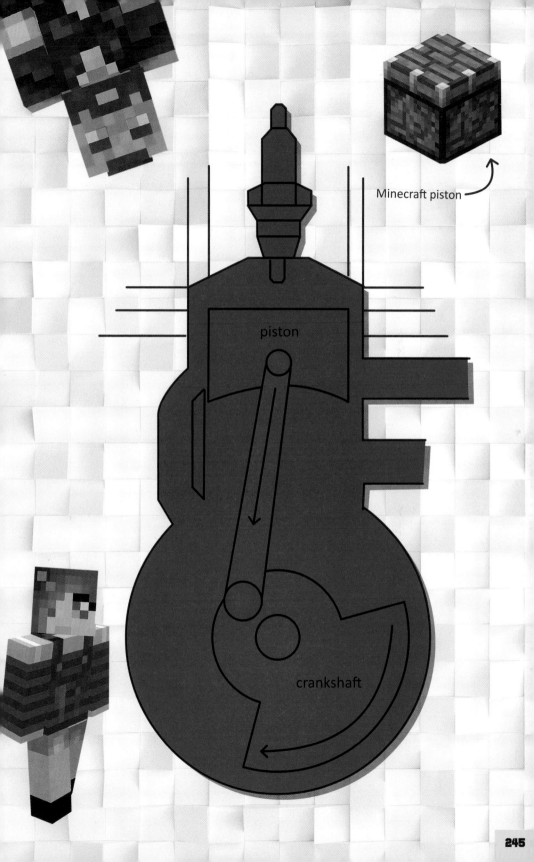

Minecraft piston

piston

crankshaft

TOP TIP!

Paintings are chosen randomly, but if you get one that's too cheerful, just remove it and try again—you might get something more sinister the next time.

STEP 5

In the dining room, remove 3x5 floor blocks in the center of the room and put pistons in their place to make a table. Then make four chairs from spruce door (for the back), red wool (for the seat) and trapdoors (for the sides). On the wall, hang some redstone torches and some paintings—the spookier the better!

In the kitchen, add a stone slab counter along one wall with crafting tables and an anvil. Add a shelf above this made from dark oak wood and trapdoors, and build more shelving to the side of this from the same materials. Opposite the counter, place four furnaces next to a sink made from a cauldron with a lever as a tap. Finally, add redstone torches, and scatter some redstone dust to the floor for gruesome decoration. Behind the iron block wall, add snow blocks to create a freezer.

Next build the stairs in the hallway. Starting eight blocks from the back wall, build your staircase up until it's four blocks high and touching the back wall, then turn the corner and build it up another four blocks. Use spruce stairs for the steps and dark oak planks and spruce fence for the sides of the stairs. Use cobblestone slabs for the landings with a sprinkling of redstone dust.

STEP 8

At the top of your stairs build a floor made of spruce wood planks. Then create a row of sleeping areas, using red sandstone, oak fence, oak wood, beds and wool. Create a storage area for your double chests using wood trapdoors and acacia doors. Finally create a window at the end of the bedroom, facing out of the front of the house. Glaze it with light-gray stained glass.

STEP 9

Before you start laying your roof, use spruce wood planks to build the walls up into central points. Then lay nether brick stairs in diagonal rows to create the roof. Knock out a cross-shaped window at the front of the house above the window and glaze it with light-gray stained glass.

Add corbels (wall supports) using cobblestone stairs. Build a balcony on the right-hand side of the house from cobblestone slabs, cobblestone stairs and spruce wood planks. Use dark oak planks, stairs, and fence to frame your windows. Frame your iron front door with cobblestone stairs, blocks and dark oak planks, and replace the cobblestone stairs at the base with nether brick stairs.

STEP 11

Finish off the grounds with mycelium, coarse dirt, sand, bushes and oak wood. You'll need to dig out the grass to put down the mycelium, dirt, and sand. And finally... go around adding some cobwebs.

⟪ JUST ADD MOBS ⟫

If you want to make your haunted house even scarier, you can spawn some terrifying zombies and skeletons inside. To make sure they stay inside, put fences over all the windows, and switch your doors for iron doors. Even then, more zombies will spawn in the park when it gets dark. To keep your visitors safe—and only scared when they're in the haunted house— add redstone lamps and daylight sensors all around the outside of the house and the perimeter of the park.

redstone torch

daylight sensor

TOP TIP!

If you want to have fun without too much fighting, select Peaceful or Low in Survival mode. Otherwise give Normal a try! If it all gets too intense, you can always switch to an easier level.

zombie

MORE ABOUT MOBS

CREEPER

These hostile and glum-looking mobs are common in Minecraft. They are silent movers and are able to sneak up on players. If creepers get within three blocks of a player they explode! Plus, if they're struck by lightning they can become charged creepers, which are stronger. Watch out!

DROWNED

Deep beneath the dolphins, coral, and tropical fish, lurks a danger for any player unlucky enough to encounter them. A drowned is a zombie that was unlucky enough to drown in water. They don't like to be on land much, and will try to find their way back to water. Stay dry to avoid them!

ENDEMITE

Although they are the smallest of the hostile mobs that spawn in Minecraft, these spooky guys should not be taken lightly. Try using a weapon enchanted with bane of anthropods to deal extra damage to them.

EVOKER

These strange creatures are incredibly powerful mobs.
They can summon flying beasts, called vexes that stop at
nothing to attack players, even swooping through walls.
Evokers can also summon giant rows of scary teeth.
Be very careful if you see them raise their arms!

GHAST

Ghasts are huge, floating mobs that live in
the Nether. They have nine tentacles and shoot
explosive reballs at the player. They are the second
largest mob that naturally spawns in the game.
Ghasts make high-pitched screams when attacking
or taking damage, and their eyes turn red.

BLAZE

The blaze is a very scary-looking mob that
spawns in Nether fortresses. They will fly
slowly toward any players they spot and
shoot out three fireballs at once! Their main
weakness is the cold, and they can be hurt
by snowballs, water, and rain.

GUARDIAN

These spiky little fish may look scary, but
they have a 40 percent chance of dropping
a perfectly sliced raw fish. Tasty! They will swim
at and attack any player (or squid!) who gets
too close. Their spikes will puff out when they
are still, but retract when they are swimming.
They can also attack with a laser, so be extra
cautious when they're around!

HUSK

What would happen to a zombie if it wandered the desert? A husk might just be the answer. They spawn in desert areas, and wander around while sometimes letting out a terrible screech. They will chase you and try to take the quickest route to you. So, if one sees you... RUN!

PHANTOM

Be sure to get plenty of sleep if you want to avoid the phantoms, as they love to chase players who have insomnia. They swoop down in groups and try to chomp you with their sharp teeth. They can hunt over large areas and will circle in the sky until they find something to attack. Yikes!

RAVAGER

Ravagers are large and very hostile mobs that spawn during raids—starting at wave three. They're described as being like an angry cow with a crossbow strapped to its head! Ravagers attack by charging into players head-first and dealing large amounts of damage. Although they can be stunned, it's best to avoid them.

SHULKER

These little box-shaped mobs can be found in End Cities. Well, that's if you're able to spot them! They are well camouflaged and can be found hiding amongst purple blocks. Get too close and they will pop open and quickly fire a homing projectile at you.

SKELETON

So long as it's dark enough, skeletons can spawn almost anywhere in Minecraft. They will chase any player that they can see! Skeletons are able to climb stairs, navigate through mazes, and even climb over some objects to get to players. They will burn up in the sun, so run into bright areas to avoid them.

SILVERFISH

These little bug-like mobs will spawn when a player breaks an infested block. If a player attacks one of these critters, silverfish can call other nearby silverfish to come and help them out. They can even see through walls, so they will find what they need very quickly!

SLIME

Strange-looking and bouncy, these odd green mobs spawn in swamps and deep underground. They can be a tricky foe. Not only can they see through walls, they can multiply. If a player kills a huge slime it will become four large slimes, each of which then turn into four small slime chunks if hit. That's a whole lot of slime!

STRAY

If you thought a skeleton was scary, just wait until you meet its icy cousin! Strays behave a lot like normal skeletons, but can also fire tipped arrows that slow you down for 30 seconds. Their melees can also slow you down. They have a creepy echo in their voice, too!

FERRIS WHEEL

A Ferris wheel is one of the star attractions of any theme park. This one gives daring passengers a great view of the water slide as they swing high in the pods.

dark blocks
show where
connecting
rows go

MATERIALS

This is what your finished Ferris wheel will look like—it will be a fun ride! You'll build it in stages:

》 the main wheel

》 the pods

》 the support structures

》 the paving and barriers

TOP TIP!

The Ferris wheel goes behind the haunted house. Look back at the plan on pages 204–5 to make sure you build it in the right place.

UNREAL!
This time, we're not starting to build on the ground but beginning in the air!

STEP 1

Your Ferris wheel is made from two parallel wheels of iron block spaced three blocks apart. Use the plan on the opposite page to help you construct the circumference and spokes of the wheel, five blocks from the ground. Then, three blocks to one side of the wheel you have just built, construct another identical wheel.

SUPPORTING ROLE

Engineers and builders have to think carefully about shape, materials, and how they support a structure as they build it.

≪ WORKING WITH IRON ≫

The main structure of the Ferris wheel is made of iron. Iron is a strong metal. It's usually made into steel, which is iron mixed with a little carbon. Steel doesn't rust, so it's better than iron for making structures like bridges (and Ferris wheels) that need to stay strong for many years. Iron was one of the earliest metals used by humans: it was first used more than 5,000 years ago.

iron block

≪ FIRST THINGS ≫ FIRST

In real life, a structure like the Ferris wheel and its pods would be delivered in parts to be bolted together on site. Real builders would construct a framework before they built the wheel—their wheel wouldn't hang in mid-air like yours!

≪ GOING IN ≫ CIRCLES

The wheel is a circle. The distance across the circle, going through the middle, is called the diameter. Half the diameter is called the radius. All the lines that go from side to side through the center of a circle are the same length.

A circle is a full turn of 360 degrees. We've divided the circle into eight equal portions, so there is an angle of 360 ÷ 8 = 45 degrees between the spokes.

Scaffolding creates a protective framework for builders, and it supports a building as it grows.

connecting rows

STEP 2

Build the 16 connecting rows that your pods will hang from, using the plan on page 259 to help you position them, and join the circles at the central axle. Attach a pod roof to the middle of each row. Make the roof from a jungle plank block surrounded by jungle wood stairs and slabs (see below). Connect the roof to the seating area with birch fence. Make the seating area from dark oak and lapiz lazuli with a birch fence safety gate. Place two jungle stairs at the bottom of the pod. Now remove the marker blocks at the base of the wheel.

marker block

STEP 3

Add some reinforcement to the wheels to stop the spokes bending out of shape. Use different colored wool to build two supporting circles on either side of your wheel. Start this six blocks out from the central hub along each vertical and horizontal beam.

SUPER STRUCTURES

The strength of a structure depends on its shape, as well as the materials it's made from. Some shapes make more stable structures than others.

« STRONG AND WEAK SHAPES »

This ancient Egyptian pyramid is strong because of its triangular shape.

A triangle is a strong shape. Pushing on one side does not easily distort the triangle. But pushing on one side of a square or rectangle can distort it into a parallelogram. Putting an extra circle inside the large circle of the Ferris wheel gives the spokes extra stability and makes it harder for the wheel to bend.

Force is spread evenly between the three sides of a triangle.

Force is spread evenly around a circle's whole shape.

Squares can be made stronger by adding a diagonal to form two triangles.

The large wheels surrounding these axles mean trains can travel further faster.

WHEELS AND AXLES

A Ferris wheel has at its heart a very simple machine, a wheel and an axle. The axle is a rod going through the center of the wheel. As the axle turns, it turns the whole wheel. While the axle turns through just a short distance, the outer edge of the wheel travels a much larger distance.

STEP 4

Now we need to anchor the wheel on the ground. Use chiseled stone bricks and purple stairs to make the two supporting legs that stretch from the ground to the hub of the wheel on each side.

STEP 5

Replace the grass blocks under the wheel with sea lanterns, so the floor glows at night! The dimensions are 24x10.

STEP 6

For lighting around the wheel, add glowstone blocks at regular intervals on both sides.

STEP 7

Dig up the grass that's left inside the area marked out for the Ferris wheel. Replace the grass with brick paving and add oak fence and cobblestone wall to make the barriers that manage the waiting line. Single stone slabs make the ideal steps up to the pods. Finish off your fence with birch leaves.

ROLLER COASTER

TOP TIP!

This is an aerial view of our roller coaster. Your track might be different, but you will need to put the landing and control booth in the same place as we have.

PLANNING

Exactly how your roller coaster looks is up to you. You can copy ours exactly, or you can design your own swoops and loops and plunges. If you want to sketch it out first, use a piece of graph paper, and draw the design you want. Then color in each square that the line crosses. This will help you to transfer your ideas to Minecraft as it converts your curve to a series of short straight lines that correspond to blocks.

No theme park is complete without a roller coaster! This one will have your customers squealing in delight as they plummet down its steep tracks. It's at the back of the theme park, towering over everything else. Let's make it the star of the show.

FAIRGROUND PHYSICS

Roller coasters thrill us, test our engineering skills and teach us more about physics than any other fairground ride. Read on to find out more...

《 FAST AND SLOW 》

A minecart traveling down a steep slope will go much more quickly than a minecart traveling down a shallow slope, and it will accelerate (speed up) as it goes. Then, as it climbs up a slope, a minecart will decelerate (slow down). Think about how to mix steep and shallow slopes to give your customers the most exciting ride.

minecart

《 DEFYING GRAVITY 》

Just like the Ferris wheel and the water slide, this build starts with a bit of building that couldn't happen in real life: setting up the basic route of the roller coaster, snaking up and down through the air, unsupported!

VELOCITY AND ACCELERATION

Real roller coaster engineers would need to think about velocity (speed) and acceleration. Velocity measures how far something travels between two points over a fixed period of time, e.g. miles per hour (mph) or feet per second (ft/s). Acceleration measures an increase in velocity. If the car gets quicker and quicker, increasing its velocity by 2 feet every second, its acceleration is 2 feet per second (written 2 ft/s). A car going at 10 ft/s that accelerates at 2 ft/s for 4 seconds, will be going at 18 ft/s by the end of that time because the velocity increases by 2 ft/s every second.

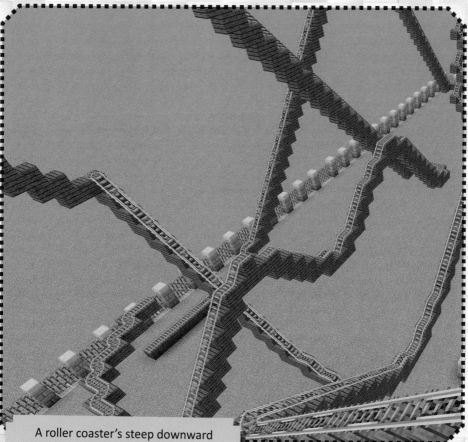

A roller coaster's steep downward slopes increase acceleration.

spirals

start
and end
of ride

STEP 1

Use spruce wood planks to trace out the route your roller coaster will follow. As long as it doesn't stretch outside the ground area allocated to the ride, it can have as many ups, downs, turns, and twists as you like. Our roller coaster has three spirals and five drops! Remember that it has to be a complete circuit, so the beginning and end must join up in a single, continuous loop. Make it just one block wide—it will be more thrilling for your customers if they're right near the edge!

MATERIALS

TOP TIP!

Your route must be solid and not have any flimsy corners, so double up the blocks underneath where necessary to make a stronger-looking base for the track.

STEP 2

Now lay track all along the top surface of the path you've made. You will need to use two types of rails: powered and unpowered rails. Use unpowered rails on downhill sections, as gravity will pull the minecarts down the slope. On uphill sections, use a mix of unpowered and powered rails. The steeper the slope, the more quickly your minecarts will slow down, so you will need more powered rails to boost them and get them to the top.

STEP 3

Each section of powered rails needs a source of power. Add oak planks, topped with a redstone torch at the start of each section of powered rails. This provides power directly to the rails, and up to nine rails connected to it.

⟪ UPS AND DOWNS ⟫

Minecraft minecarts behave differently on powered and unpowered rails.

On unpowered rails, a minecart moves if it is pushed forward or if gravity pulls it downward. If a minecart has to move uphill, it slows down and eventually stops, as it runs out of momentum.

On powered rails that are turned on, a minecart will move forward, even uphill. But if the powered rail is turned off, it slows down any minecarts moving along it. This means you need powered track to boost your minecarts to get up the slopes and then unpowered track lets them whiz down freely, relying on gravity.

minecart

powered rail

Skateboarders use momentum to reach the top of ramps.

MOMENTUM AND FRICTION

A moving object has momentum—it keeps moving in the same direction. If you push a toy car across the floor, it will keep going until it stops naturally, or until it runs into something.

The reason the toy car stops naturally after a while is because the wheels of the car and the floor rub against each other—this is called friction.

The smoother two surfaces are, the less friction occurs between them.

You slip on ice because it's very smooth, so there is little friction between the ice and your shoes. You aren't likely to slip on gravel as there is a lot of friction between that surface and your shoes.

On a roller coaster, the speed the car gains traveling downhill gives it enough momentum to get up at least part of the next slope. Momentum won't carry it far, though, so you will need powered rails for a longer uphill ride.

This roller coaster train gains momentum as it drops down a slope.

STEP 4

A ride that just hangs in the air looks unstable and will be way too scary! Let's add some supports to hold the track up. Use oak fence to fill in all the gaps between the track and the ground, adding oak wood columns with a gap of five blocks between each. Now it's starting to look more like a roller coaster!

STEP 5

Safety is important on a roller coaster. Add a total of four access poles made from columns of oak wood around the roller coaster's upward and downward spirals. Next to the start of the ride, connect the access poles to the roller coaster with oak fence. Add powered rails to give the minecarts an extra push as they level out at the top of the upward spiral.

Redstone comparators are blocks that can maintain, compare, or subtract signal strength in a redstone circuit.

STEP 6

Next to the start of the ride, dig a pit. In the pit, put a redstone comparator, an oak pressure plate, and a redstone torch. Connect them all up to the rails with redstone wire. Then cover everything with grass and put back the section of track you removed. Then, when the customer treads on the pressure plate, it cancels the signal to the comparator. This makes the cart go backwards round the curve, and then move back on to the roller coaster ride where it can be used again by another customer.

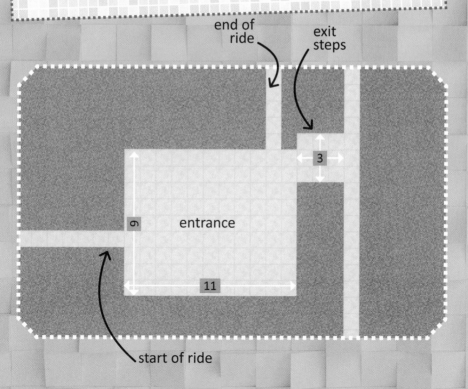

end of ride

exit steps

3

9

entrance

11

start of ride

FAIRGROUND PHYSICS

《 POWERING UP 》

Electricity can only flow through a completed circuit. A circuit needs a source of power (such as a battery or powerlines), and wires to conduct electricity. Wires connect the source of power to the device that will do work in the circuit—like a light bulb, or a buzzer.

As soon as the components are connected, electricity flows and the light comes on, or the buzzer makes a noise. You can add a switch to make it easy to stop and start the flow of electricity. The switch works by breaking the circuit (when it's turned off) and completing the circuit (when it's turned on). In the roller coaster, you need to stop the cars moving so that people can get in or out, so a switch is vital.

redstone repeater

redstone block

daylight sensor

redstone wire

redstone torch

oak pressure plate

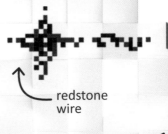

WHEELS ON ROADS AND RAILS

If you look at the tires of a bicycle or car, you will see that they have a pattern on them, called tread. This increases the friction with the road surface so that the wheels don't slide around, especially when it's wet. When a vehicle goes on rails, engineers aim for as little friction as possible between the wheels and the rails. At the same time, it's important that the wheels stay on the rails. The solution is wheels with flanges. The flange sticks down on one side of the wheel, so that side can't lift up and go over the rail. Since there are flanges on opposite sides of each pair of wheels, the vehicle can't easily fall to either side.

The flange on the edge of this steam train wheel keeps it on the track.

minecart

STEP 7

With all the track in place, it's time to build the entrance where people will get into the minecarts. Build this over the top of the control panel you've just made. Use jungle wood planks for the walls, spruce stairs for seating on the other side of the track, and spruce slabs for the roof. Complete it with cobblestone wall columns at the front, and a stone button on the central column at the back that you can press to start the ride.

STEP 8

Use stone slabs and bricks to pave the ground. Add oak fence and organize the waiting-line area. This is going to be a popular ride, so we've set aside a large area for people to wait. Make sure alternate rows of fence go right to the wall to stop eager customers from cutting in line! At the end of the ride, create an exit path starting with oak wood stair steps and edged with cobblestone wall. Finally, add minecarts to the track.

ANIMAL ZONE

A theme park can be a bit overstimulating with all those exciting rides, so how about giving your customers somewhere calming to relax? The animal zone is just that—a place to chill with some friendly beasts.

MATERIALS

« ZOO OVERVIEW »

Here's the basic layout for the animal zone. Each enclosure is rectangular, but otherwise it is adapted to suit the needs of the type of animal that will live in it.

NATURAL SELECTION

We've used farm animals, but you could pick different animals and change the enclosures to suit your choices.

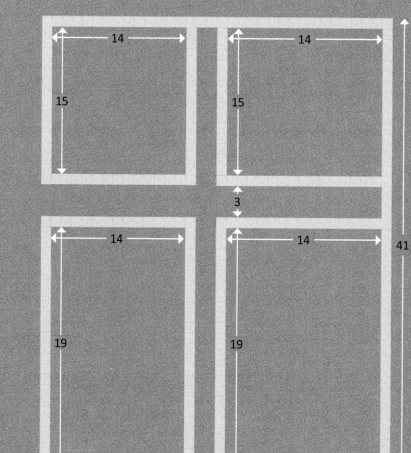

14

15

14

15

41

3

14

19

14

19

34

≪ ROOM WITH ≫ A MOO

There will be two larger enclosures, one for the horses and one for the cows, and two slightly smaller areas, one for the sheep and chickens, and one for the rabbits.

《 PLANNING FOR LIFE 》

All the other builds have been planned to make it fun, safe, and easy for visitors to use the theme park. But animals are living things too, so we must take their needs into account. They all need:

» food

» water

» a safe, dry place to live.

But different types of animals also have specific needs. They need different environments (surroundings) that reflect the places they are usually found in the wild, and different types of food. You wouldn't keep polar bears and lions in the same type of environment, for example. Lions live in the hot grasslands of Africa, but polar bears live in the cold snow and ice of countries near the North Pole.

fish

raw beef

hay bale

water bucket

TOP TIP!

In Survival mode, mobs sometimes escape through fence. Keep the same look but improve security by adding a layer of glass panes around the outside of your fence.

glass pane

≪ LOOK OUT! ≫

Some animals eat other animals and are fierce predators. It's safe to mix some types of animals, but others might hurt each other, either on purpose or accidentally. You also need to make sure your animals will be kept safely enclosed by the barriers you use. You don't want them wandering all over the theme park!

STEP 1

Start by laying rows of mossy cobblestone wall to mark out the walls of all four enclosures. Use the plan on page 289 for the positions of the cobblestone wall.

STEP 2

Complete the walls of the horse enclosure using mossy cobblestone wall. Build them four blocks high, with columns placed five blocks apart. Create a pattern by leaving two sections of wall hanging down and one pointing up between each column. These gaps allow people to see the animals from outside.

STEP 3

Build the walls for the rabbit enclosure from mossy cobblestone wall four blocks high, too, but with columns placed three blocks apart. Between these columns, remove T-shaped sections of your wall to create viewing windows.

STEP 4

Construct the walls for the sheep and chicken enclosure by placing mossy cobblestone wall in a zigzag pattern. Make each diagonal zig (or zag!) four blocks high and three blocks across. When you're done there should be lots of upside down, T-shaped viewing windows.

STEP 5

Space the columns in the walls of the cow enclosure two blocks apart, with lazy figure-of-eight shapes removed to make the viewing windows.

FOOD AND FEEDING

All living things need food, and at the bottom of the food chain, supporting everything, are plants. Learn how to grow them, and you'll be able to look after all your animals.

« HAY FOR HERBIVORES »

Most of the animals in the animal zone are herbivores: that means that they eat plants. Lots of animals are herbivores, including many mammals, birds, insects, and fish. Elephants, squirrels, parrots, snails, and caterpillars are all herbivores. They eat leaves, fruit, nuts, and seeds from plants. Other animals eat meat— other animals. They are called carnivores. Lions, dogs, sharks, and vultures are carnivores. And some animals can eat plants or animals. They are called omnivores. Pigs and some monkeys are omnivores.

hay bale

ENTER THE ANIMALS!

In Minecraft, all animals can be spawned from one of their spawn eggs, but in real life animals either give birth to live babies or lay eggs. Birds and reptiles lay eggs. Most mammals give birth to babies. Some fish give birth and others lay eggs.

spawn egg

GROWING PLANTS

Plants need several things to grow well. They need water, sunlight, and soil with the right kind of nutrients. To help plants to grow, farmers and gardeners often add fertilizer to the soil. This works like extra food for the plants. One type of fertilizer is bone meal, made of ground-up animal bones. Bones are rich in the element phosphorous, which is vital for plants.

poppy

BABY GROWTH

Some baby animals can eat the same food as adult animals as soon as they are born or hatched. Mammals produce milk to feed their young. Other animals chew up or partly digest food before feeding it to their babies. Lots of birds do this.

It's no use having an enclosure that no one can get into! Put a gate in the wall of each enclosure using dark oak fence gates. It should be three blocks in from the crossroads at the center of the animal zone. Leave space above the gate for head room so that people can fit through!

STEP 7

Horses eat hay, so pile some hay bales up in one corner of their enclosure. And, like all animals, horses need fresh water to drink. Put three troughs in another corner and fill them with water. Then spawn your horses!

STEP 8

Next to the horse enclosure, build two chicken coops, using birch wood for the walls, and oak stairs for the roof. Add a row of birch stairs across the bottom of the coops to keep the chickens off the ground at night. Don't forget an oak door so it's easy for park workers to go inside and clean the chicken coops. Add birch planks above it for decoration. The sheep and chickens need water to drink. Dig a pond (just two blocks deep so that it's not too dangerous) and edge it with some blocks of sand, set into the ground. Finally, sprinkle some bone meal to make the grass and some extra flowers grow. Then spawn your sheep and chickens.

TOP TIP!

Feed your chickens watermelon, wheat, or pumpkin seeds, and shut them away in their coop at night to keep them safe!

TIME TO REPRODUCE

Happy, well-fed animals will eventually start to make babies. Different types of animals do this in different ways, in the real world as well as in Minecraft...

« BIRDS VS MAMMALS »

Although real chickens come from eggs, cows, sheep, horses, and rabbits are all mammals. Mammals carry their babies inside them and give birth to them. Birds, reptiles, and some types of fish lay eggs.

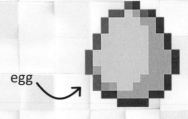

egg

THE RIGHT ENVIRONMENT

Minecraft mobs, just like real animals, reproduce in particular places. For example, horses naturally spawn in savannas or plains. Wolves only spawn in taiga biomes, and polar bears, as you'd imagine, spawn in ice plains. Cows, pigs, and chickens are pretty common and pop up all over the place.

In the real world, things are pretty similar, cold places with little food, like the Arctic, have fewer animals while warm places with lots of vegetation, like the Amazon, are host to lots of animal species.

GOOD BREEDING

To encourage passive or tame mobs to breed, offer them food. When heart particles appear, mobs are in love mode. Two animals of the same type will come together as long as they are not more than eight blocks apart. Then, after a few seconds, a baby of the same type will appear.

In the real world, animals tend to breed in spring or the start of the rainy season when warmer weather is on the way and plants are starting to grow. Warmth and food give their young a better chance of surviving.

Minecraft river biomes are a great place to fish.

STEP 9

The next big enclosure is for cows. This has some landscaping, with a bit of higher ground and a tree. The cows will need a lot to drink, so dig a hole to set six troughs into the ground and fill them with water. To make the raised area, use grass blocks piled up, and sprinkle some bone meal to add tall grass and flowers to the ground. Finally, spawn your cows.

bone meal

TOP TIP!

If you sprinkle bone meal over grass, it makes the grass grow taller (and flowers grow, too). This is very important for the sheep and chicken enclosure because sheep turn grass to dirt when they graze, so you'll need to keep sprinkling bone meal there.

STEP 10

Prepare the rabbit enclosure by adding some jungle wood with jungle leaves over the top of it to create some bushes where they can shelter. Dig a pond in one corner and fill it with water so that they can have a drink. Spawn your bunnies and then tap (or right click) the grass with your shovel to create paths between the enclosures.

STEP 11

Sprinkle bone meal to grow flowers and tall grass. These will provide food for your bunnies, as well as somewhere for them to hide.

FOR REAL!

Fertilizer makes plants grow faster in the real world. In Minecraft you can use bone meal to make saplings grow faster.

ANIMALS

IN MINECRAFT

Get the lowdown on the various creatures you may meet in your Minecraft adventures...

BAT

These tiny flying creatures LOVE the dark and will spawn in caves and other dark places. Sometimes they fly into lava and catch fire, so look out when exploring underground! They have a loud squeak too.

CAT

Cats are cute animals that spawn as strays in villages. They don't take fall damage but it is still best to avoid very big heights. Phantoms and creepers hate cats, so they're handy to have around!

CHICKEN

They may spend most of their time wandering around aimlessly, but chickens like to be in the light. They also like to follow players with certain types of seed. Chickens will lay an egg every five to ten minutes.

PIG

Pigs are a very common animal in Minecraft and tend to spawn in grassy areas where there is plenty of daylight. Pigs can look silly sometimes as they often try to jump onto objects that are too big for them!

FOX

Foxes are nocturnal mobs, which means that they come out at night. The good news is that foxes are passive, so they run away from players rather than attacking them! Foxes love to hunt chickens, rabbits, and baby turtles.

SPIDER

Be careful around these scary little creatures! They hang around in dark places and try to attack you, so make sure you carry defenses or be prepared to run! They are the only animal in Minecraft that can climb walls.

MULE

Just like a horse or a donkey, the mule can be used to carry items and help the player to move a lot of items quickly. Mules don't spawn naturally in Minecraft, but they are the result of breeding a horse with a donkey.

DOLPHIN

Dolphins are very intelligent and curious animals, and will try to have fun and games with you if they can see you. They can be found swimming in the ocean in large groups and sometimes leaping out of the water. Dolphins defend each other, so be careful not to hurt them!

FINISHING TOUCHES

THEME PARK

All your rides are ready, but before the park opens for business you need to add some finishing touches. We'll add paving, lighting, a ticket booth, a large entrance sign— and make sure people can get into and out of the rides!

≪ THINKING ABOUT ROUTES ≫

When you have a lot of people milling around in an area, they need to be able to move to where they want to go without getting in each others' way. The entrances and exits are separate to keep people moving smoothly and safely.

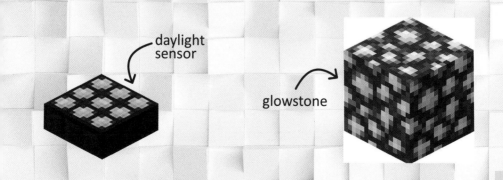

NIGHT LIGHTS

Glowstone provides light during Minecraft's night. In the real world, substances that glow on their own in the dark are known as "phosphorescent." They absorb and store light, then release it.

Solar powered lights have a solar panel which absorbs energy from sunlight during the day. This solar energy is stored in a battery. A light sensor monitors the sunlight and triggers a switch when it goes above or below a certain level. When it gets dark, the solar powered lights turn on, using power from the battery. Some lights powered by household electricity come on automatically at night, either using a light sensor or a timer.

Many different types of sensors are used to trigger automatic reactions. Security lights and car alarms have motion sensors: if something moves near the light, it turns on, or if the car is bumped or pushed, the alarm sounds. Smoke detectors have a sensor that sets off an alarm if there is smoke in the air.

daylight sensor

glowstone

STEP 1

First pave the central path inside the theme park with diorite. So far, the ground here is still covered with grass, but in a real park that would soon get turned to mud when hoards of eager customers rush in. The paved area runs from the entrance to behind the haunted house.

STEP 2

Around the edges of your path, add a row of andesite and glowstone blocks. Placing the glowstone every six blocks will provide ground-level lighting at night.

STEP 3

Now go around the whole of the path, adding entrances and exits for all the rides with glowstone blocks either side. The exit for the bouncy castle goes next to the grass that runs in front of the landing area. The entrances and exits for the other rides connect with the waiting-line areas and paths. We've marked where these go on the image below.

entrance

STEP 4

Now people can find their way safely along the paths. Let's add some torches so that they can see clearly when they are waiting in line. Plant a torch on the end of each bit of fence in the waiting-line areas; add extras if you like.

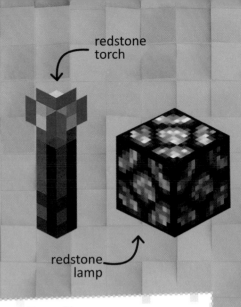

redstone torch

redstone lamp

STEP 5

We need a ticket booth so that people visiting the park can pay to come in. Place it in a central position at the front entrance. Make it seven blocks wide and six blocks from back to front, with stone brick walls and a roof made from spruce wood stairs. Put a single row of andesite around the base. Add dark oak fence on either side up to the edge of the path.

painting

sign

STEP 6

Now add side windows, using glass panes. To make it nicer for the person who has to work in the ticket booth, add a painting to the wall. Then place a villager inside.

TOP TIP!

At the main entrance, use signs to direct your guests toward the different attractions in the theme park. Then, outside the entrance to each attraction, put a sign with a fun name on it!

STEP 7

Finish off the theme park with a huge sign near the entrance. Make it really big so that people can see it from a long way away, and it will draw in customers. This one is 30 blocks high and 24 blocks wide. Make the supports and the face of the sign from black stained clay and the frame from yellow wool. We've left the face of this sign blank so you can create your own name for it—it's your park, so make your mark on it! Use more brightly colored wool to make your lettering.

THEME PARK

Finally, sprinkle bone meal to add some flowers around the rides or along the fences. Or maybe you'd like to add a few benches, more trees, or more lighting. If you want to add more rides, you could take down part of the perimeter fence and extend the park. Your park could grow and grow!

dandelion

oak sapling

poppy

tall grass

tree

sunflower

GLOSSARY

ABSORB
To take in.

ACCELERATION
The process of getting steadily faster, building up speed.

ACCOMMODATE
Providing a place to live, or a space to store something.

AIR CONDITIONING
A system that keeps a building cool.

ANTENNAE
An aerial for receiving radio signals.

ARCHITECT
A person whose job is to design buildings and build structures, such as bridges.

ATRIUM
A space inside a building that's open-air or covered with a skylight.

CENTURY
A period of 100 years.

CIRCUIT
A closed loop of wire and other components that conduct electricity, so that a current can flow and the electricity can be used to do useful work, such as power lights.

CIRCUMFERENCE
The length of the edge of a circle.

COBWEBS
Type of block in Minecraft that can be found in strongholds or abandoned mine shafts.

CONDUCT (ELECTRICITY, HEAT)
To carry.

CORBEL
A structural piece of stone on a wall.

CONSTRUCTION
The process of building something—usually a large structure.

CRANKSHAFT
The part of a machine that connects to a piston, converting the backward-and-forward motion of the piston to a circular motion.

CUBOID
Box-shaped object with six flat sides. All angles are right angles.

CYLINDER
A tube-shaped container.

DIAMETER
A line across a circle, through the center, dividing it in half.

DIMENSIONS
Measurements (e.g. on a plan).

DISTORT
To stretch something out of shape.

DUPLICATE
To create an exact copy of something so that it is identical to the first.

EARTHQUAKE
A movement of the ground caused by events deep in the Earth.

ELECTROMAGNETIC
Magnetic field created by an electric current.

ELECTROMAGNETIC WAVES
Waves that travel through space (or matter) including radio waves, visible light waves, and microwaves.

ENVIRONMENT
The natural setting in which something lives or is situated. It can refer to a local environment (such as a forest or lake) or the whole natural world, often called "the environment."

EQUILATERAL TRIANGLE
A triangle with internal angles of the same size.

EXCAVATE
To dig up and out of the ground.

FLAMMABLE
Capable of being burned.

FOOD CHAIN
A series of organisms (living things) that eat one another. For example, a fox eats a rabbit which in turn eats grass.

FOOTPRINT
The area on the ground occupied or overhung by a building.

FOUNDATION
Underground support for a building or other structure.

FRICTION
A force that prevents or slows down the movement of one surface over another.

HYDRAULIC
Powered by a system of compressed fluids (liquid or gas).

INSULATION
Material that doesn't carry heat, used to keep something warm (because the heat is trapped).

ISOSCELES TRIANGLES
A triangle with two equal sides, and two angles the same size.

LAPIS LAZULI
Metamorphic rock and semi-precious stone with a deep blue color.

MAGENTA
A purplish-pink color.

MALWARE
Software that has been designed to damage a computer.

MICROWAVES
A form of electromagnetic radiation, often used for heating up food.

MOMENTUM
The ability of a moving object to keep moving unless some force or object stops it.

OCTAGON
A shape with eight straight sides.

OPAQUE
Material that you are not able to see through.

PARALLELOGRAM
A four-sided shape with opposite sides that are parallel and the same length as each other.

PENTHOUSE
Luxurious and expensive apartment on the top floor of a building.

PERIMETER
The total distance around the edge(s) of a shape.

PRISM
Three-dimensional shape with identical ends (bases) and flat sides (faces).

PROPORTIONS
The same relative sizes of two measurements. For example, if a rectangle is twice as long as it is tall in a plan, the corresponding rectangle in a model must also be twice as long as it is tall.

RADIUS
A line from the center of a circle to the edge (circumference).

RUBBLE
Small rocks and pieces of stone.

SCALE
The relationship between the size of something to its size in a plan. A scale of 1:100 means one unit (1 in) on a plan stands for 100 units (1 ft) of the building.

SENSOR
A device that detects movement sound, light, or temperature.

SKYSCRAPER
A very tall building.

SOLAR PANEL
A panel of solar cells which converts sunlight to electricity.

SOLAR POWERED
Driven with electricity converted from the energy in sunlight.

SOUNDPROOFING
Material used to stop sound.

SPECTRUM
Band of colors that appear in the rainbow and combine to make white light.

STIMULUS
Something (such as sound, light, or heat) that causes a reaction.

STORY
A floor (level) in a building.

STRUTS
Supports that strengthen a building or structure.

SYMMETRY
An object that has the identical size, shape, and position of parts on opposite sides of a dividing line, plane, or point.

TESSELLATE
To fit together in a regular pattern with no gaps left in between.

TRANSLUCENT
Objects or material that lets some light pass through it.

TRENCH
Narrow and long ditch in the ground.

VELOCITY
Speed.

VIEWING PLATFORM
A place to stand to see a long way, or overlook a particular place.

VIRUS
Digital code that can copy itself and corrupt systems or data.

WATER-TIGHT
Capable of keeping water in or out without leaking.

X-RAY
A form of electromagnetic radiation, often used for looking inside the body.